The Biography
of
Little Johnny L. Mitchell

The Biography *of* Little Johnny L. Mitchell

Written and illustrated by
BILL PRICE

RESOURCE *Publications* • Eugene, Oregon

THE BIOGRAPHY OF LITTLE JOHNNY L. MITCHELL

Resource Publications
An Imprint of Wipf and Stock Publishers
199 W. 8th Ave., Suite 3
Eugene, OR 97401

www.wipfandstock.com

PAPERBACK ISBN: 979-8-3852-7309-6
HARDCOVER ISBN: 979-8-3852-7310-2
EBOOK ISBN: 979-8-3852-7311-9

VERSION NUMBER 022526

To all my students who knew me as Mr. Price,
but didn't know the real me!

Contents

Introduction | 1

Chapter 1
Breaking up is Hard | 4

Chapter 2
Family One and Learning from Spankings | 10

Chapter 3
Family Two and The TV | 15

Chapter 4
The Care-less family, the Bees, and the Bite. | 23

Chapter 5
Family Four and the Unthinkable | 30

Chapter 6
Bad Paint | 36

Chapter 7
The Final Foster Family | 43

Chapter 8
A New Home—A New Family | 53

Chapter 9
The First Day | 58

Chapter 10
Yes, Billy, There is a Santa | 66

Chapter 11
Change Brings About Change | 73

Chapter 12
A Christmas to Remember | 77

Chapter Final
The Day That Changed his World | 82

Appendix | 87

About the Author | 89

Introduction

FAMILY STRUCTURE IS NOT always structured. Normally a family is divided into separate roles. There are parents or a parent who, traditionally, rule the roost. They are in charge and are expected to create a learning environment in which the other members, no matter how many, thrive. Parents, generally, set the rules which should be followed basically to create a safe space for everyone involved. Traditional family parents show each other and any children they have a special kind of love not found outside the home. There is a unity caused by a connection because they all carry, more or less, the same genes. I am not saying here that everything is always peace and love, because there is fighting, disagreements, and times of anger. Somehow, though, they always seem to come together as a unit.

There are other members of family units that do not, however, always follow the formula for a successful family. Power plays a big role. Invariably a child grows up and starts to spread his or her wings, as it were. At a certain age the children, in one form or another, rebel and depending on the situation conflict evolves. Many times the problem is resolved and sometimes there seems to be no resolution.

Simply because there are brothers and sisters who are connected in the family structure, doesn't means that there is no conflict. It seems sometimes that not one average family can survive a day without it. Brother fights brother, sister fights sister, children fight with parents, and parents are not guiltless either. These struggles usually work themselves out, though, either with love or a few sibling bruises here or there. This, in every way, is normal. It is the definition of an everyday stereotypical family.

Not all families are stereotypical. Not all children grow with the pleasures and pains found in conventional family relationships. Some children find themselves in a situation not of their own making. Some loose the family structure and are required to be raised by others. These other people may mean well, and they may be accepting this responsibility of caring for a child, who isn't theirs, for all the right reasons. Not all adults, however, fall into this category.

There were monetary reasons for accepting children who have come from a torn family. In some cases, it isn't done out of love. When this happens no one wins, especially a young child. That child may grow up feeling unwanted and unloved. These children soon understand that they are in a situation that is out of the norm. Some of them are placed with adults who, because of requirements, give little more than is necessary for survival. Some of these children know nothing about holidays, birthdays, or any other special days. One of these unfortunate children was little Johnny L. Mitchell.

As a matter of fact, birthdays as far as Johnny knew were for good kids and he knew he was not going to be given the chance to celebrate his. Other unfortunate boys and girls, in the same situation as Johnny, receive no gifts to unwrap and had no birthday cake or ice cream to enjoy. Some were, maybe, given a candy bar and told to be satisfied with it. Sometimes a halfhearted happy birthday would follow. Most of the time though, there was no celebration, or the day was not even mentioned. Children got up, went about their duties as a kid, and went to bed with not a mention of the importance of the day. To be truthful, Johnny L. Mitchell didn't even know the date of his own birthday.

Christmas, too, was like birthdays in that some kids, including Johnny, would not have been able to celebrate. Little Johnny knew Santa wouldn't visit on Christmas eve. Even at the age of four and five, he understood there would be nothing under a tree or in a stocking for him, at least not a new toy. He did receive toys that he recognized on more than one occasion. He knew they were old though, because he had seen them before, in the hands of older foster kids who had since moved on. Most of the time there was nothing and, between the ages of four and eight, Johnny would not believe in Christmas at all. The reason for this was that Johnny L. Mitchell was not a member of a traditional family and when it came to any celebrations, he was not included.

He hadn't been a member of a real time-honored family since he turned four. Yes, he had lived with foster parents, many of them. As a matter of fact, there had been six families in four years. Oh, he was fed enough to survive and had a place out of the rain most of the time, but there was no security or real love to be had. He knew he was never in a real home and, certainly, there was never ever a real family he could feel a part of. On every day of his life his memory about his birth family seemed to fade or he would purposely forget because of pain. He would, once in a while, think about his real family and his eyes would well up, He would then try to forget so it wouldn't hurt so much He would never forget, however, how it all started.

Chapter 1

Breaking up is Hard

It was freezing when Johnny L. Mitchell was born in the city of Baltimore. No one would see this as a foreshadowing of things to come, but it may well have been. It was on a cold January day in nineteen fifty-four when his mother held him in her arms for the first time. He was the newest of what would eventually turn out to be a household of nine children; he was a part of a large nineteen-fifties family.

In those days, families were, many times, much larger than the families of the twenty first century. The typical family consisted of a father, who worked to support the household, and a mother who stayed at home and took care of the children, cooked, and made sure the house was running

efficiently. Each member of the family was responsible for helping to make the family unit work. Usually, the private life of the family was never discussed in public. Public and private were separate and the predominance of children born in the fifties, were members of such a family.

Today the family unit is far different. Many children are now being raised by a single mother and many of those mothers are not married. Some kids live with a single father and some are raised by grandparents with no parents at all. Some now live with two mothers or two fathers. The twenty-first century household calls this a diverse family unit, but in the nineteen fifties this would, in most cases, just not be found.

The Mitchell family, itself, was typical and was loving, with a father who worked as hard as he could to make sure his children and his wife didn't go without the things that were needed. The children knew they couldn't have everything they wanted, because that would be unquestionably selfish and families just weren't that way.

This particular typical family had a mother, too, who was quick to laugh and even quicker to love. Johnny's mother would make sure everyone was treated fairly and each child knew that she loved them just as much as the others. She was kind, but she was also strict. What she said was to be done. She taught the children to do what was required of them and to do it with a smile, if possible. If not, do it anyway. That is how it was always done.

Although Johnny was too young at the time to realize what kind of family he had been born into, somehow, he could sense the love and caring. He was happy as a part of a family with a mother who spent the day taking care of the children and trying to bring them up to become the best they could be. Her days were filled with washing and cleaning and cooking, all while listening to each child's shouts and cries and constant questions. It was she, too, that taught them the meaning of family and showed each one that her love was equal among all of them. There were fights and quarrels and there were many differences of opinions just as every family faced, but there was an incredible sense of love. That was the one obvious thing that could be seen by everyone. Even when there wasn't enough for any of the extras, there was so much love to go around that Johnny had another sister when he was only two and the entire family celebrated and was genuinely happy.

They didn't have a lot of money, and they all knew that, but they more than made up for that with love. Everyone looked after everyone else. Brothers and sisters would fight and argue, just as every other brother and sister who was a part of a large family would. But, if a problem arose, they worked together to solve it.

If there was a situation that affected one brother or sister, all the others would join in and defend that sibling. Obviously, Johnny was too young to understand it all, but he did know what love was and he could feel the security found within the family.

Play was good too. The children would get involved in games so that everyone was included. Even Johnny and his new sister were involved in some way, and the others made sure of that. It may have been a time when Johnny was allowed to join in when the older children were playing kickball. He was allowed to kick the ball, even if it didn't go but a few feet in front of him. The others would still cheer for him. It wasn't just play time that was fun for Johnny. He could remember when he would sit on his older sister's lap and clap as the others would sing together around the dining room table. There were times when one older sibling would sit quietly with Johnny and play "Candy Land" or "Chutes and Ladders", even though they knew Johnny didn't always understand the game. They would help him move his piece to the proper position, counting as they moved. It didn't matter what was being done, it was the fact that it was being done together.

Even though the family was close knit and everyone always worked through most every problem that would arise, Johnny's father never really talked about himself, especially when it came to his health. He was not well and everyone knew it. He had this thing they called epilepsy and little was known, at the time, about this neurological disorder. All people saw were the affects. There were sometimes episodes of strange behavior, weird feelings and at times there was a complete loss of consciousness. Some people with epilepsy might just stare for a few seconds during a seizure, while others jerked their bodies repeatedly and maybe become unconscious. Mr. Mitchell would sometimes experience the worst part. Many people did not understand this disease and their attitude toward the infected person was often negative. If they witnessed an epileptic "fit", as it was often called, and they would shun the person affected and treat him or her as an outcast.

At first, for Mr. Mitchell, it was under control and working was no problem for him. He would have an episode once in a great while, and the family always knew what to expect. Others however, were afraid of the sight. Not many people knew what to do in the case of someone experiencing a seizure.

In the fifties, epilepsy didn't have the organization that exists now. It was, in fact, in the1950s when the Epilepsy Associations were started, but those affected were still discriminated against. It was only after many of these Associations were created that public awareness was expanded and social and medical changes began. There were improvements, but not in time for Mr. Mitchell.

Everything would have been wonderful if things in Johnny's world had never changed. He would have grown to understand that blood was thicker than water and family was more important than any other relationships. He would have been taught that family sticks together no matter what. Love was the glue and his family understood that. But, as things happen in an uncertain world, situations change. When the Mitchell family least expected it, bad things got worse, and that is when life taught them a lesson. Sometimes glue breaks; it is not the love that is gone, it just happens that circumstances change things for families.

One summer afternoon Johnny's father took a turn for the worse. He began to have epileptic seizures more often and that affected everything. He started missing work and eventually lost his job. Because he was never sure of what would happen to him, and because the seizures continued and grew more severe, Johnny's dad could not find work. No one in that era would hire someone who could cause problems in the workplace. Those who hired, would not think of employing someone who may have a seizure during work hours, thereby disrupting the entire day. If Mr. Mitchell had taken a job and not told them about his illness, then, if he had an episode while at work, he would have been fired immediately. Back then anyone could be fired for any reason and no explanation was needed.

The doctors, too, said that there was little they could do. There were medicines which helped some, but Johnny's father found nothing to ease his pain and seizures. There were those who were researching possible epilepsy relief by examining the temporal lobe of the brain, but neuroscience was just beginning. In the 1970's anti-seizure medications were developed and around two-thirds of those affected could find relief. Today, doctors can use machines to determine where the epilepsy is found in the brain. Newer research shows doctors whether the seizures center in the temporal or frontal lobes, and new medicines are now available to help control seizures. None of this, however, was accessible to Mr. Mitchell.

Soon the money just wasn't there and change was inevitability. The family struggled to make ends meet. They gave up the many things they were used to and, despite the daily problems, they tried to make it work. They all shared and they all made the things they did have stretch a bit further, but Johnny's father admitted that love and sharing didn't put meat on the table. Little by little the entire family began feeling the pressure and the depression. The family had changed and tensions were stretched.

Johnny was four when his natural parents came to the decision that they could no longer take care of their nine children. They wanted everything to work, but Mr. Mitchell's epilepsy and constant attacks, the lack of a job, and the absence of money made the decision for the both of them. Although Johnny's mom did her best to help him and keep the family together, there was nothing left to do; they were fighting a lost cause. Something had to be done before the children went to bed every night hungry. It was then, and only then, that Johnny's parents met with social services and the decision was finalized. In the fifties, just as it is today, no one would invite nine children into their home; as many understood it, that would be insanity.

Gradually, one by one, the family was divided. The first-time foster care found a home for one of the children, tears flowed and an emptiness took over. Tears and fears soon were a daily occurrence for the children. Every time another child would leave for a foster home, the breaking up of the family would take away a piece of something inside. Johnny was one of the last to leave. By the time the Service had found him a foster home, it seemed that almost all emotion had left him. He no longer felt much, because not feeling much - didn't hurt. Johnny's foster care lady, named Mrs. Troxel, was a sweet lady and cared for others, but that didn't enter the minds of those who were affected by the moves that were happening to the Mitchell family. Johnny could actually sense the sadness being felt by all, but could also feel the pain of fear caused by the unknown.

Chapter 2

Family One and Learning from Spankings

JOHNNY WAS TAKEN FROM the arms of his mother when he was four years old. He took a look in her eyes and saw that she was purposely holding back tears. Nothing could, however, hide the wetness welling up in them. She had said it was all for the best and that everything was going to turn out for the good. After all, there was no other choice. Johnny was crying as he was led out to the foster worker's car. His arms remained outstretched as if this act would change minds and he would return to his mommy's arms. He was placed in the back seat and all he could do was look out of tear-filled eyes at the home he was losing.

Soon, his shirt sleeves dried his tears and he sat quietly in the back seat of the car as the social worker took him to meet a new family. He watched row house after row house disappear as they traveled away from the only life he knew. His stomach was turning upside down and he felt so sick. He thought this feeling would never leave him; there was nothing he could do or say.

At the time it didn't mean much, because Johnny was too young to know what was really going on. All he knew was everything was changing. However, children learn very quickly and Johnny was a quick study, even at this early age. He was, though, about to learn the difference between natural families and foster families.

Johnny's first foster family was something he had never experienced before. They believed that sparing the rod would spoil the child. They also believed that alcohol solved most problems. The use of a few drinks certainly made foster parenting bearable to them. They talked a good talk, and had convinced the social workers that they had nothing but love and room to help unfortunate children. They had explained the God himself had taught them to look out for those less fortunate than they. Assuring the social worker a boy of Johnny's age would do nothing but improve and grow to become an upstanding citizen, if that child were left in their care. And it worked. They had been chosen to accept Little Johnny into their home.

It was a good enough house, in a good enough neighborhood. Johnny noticed, though, how every home looked like every other home. Every set of steps were the same, all whitish and all of equal size and shape. All of the houses were made of similar red bricks and Johnny heard people say it was called the brick jungle. The front door looked like all the other front doors and Johnny wondered how people knew their house from the neighbor's house. The door led to the living room, which according to these people would still be called a parlor. In back of that was the dining room, followed by the kitchen. Everything was neat. There wasn't a mess anywhere. There were no toys left on the floor and not a speck of dust was around. Johnny guessed cleaning must have been done every day or maybe even twice a day.

At the end of the parlor, a set of wooden stairs led to the second floor and that led to the bedrooms. Johnny was taken up to what would become his room and he saw that this, too, was just as neat and clean and staunch as the first room he had seen. He liked the windows though. There were three of them. One was placed on a flat wall. There were two more that were placed in a little rounded alcove where he would be able to sit and watch whatever was going on outside. His new parents, with a smile that Johnny thought wasn't a smile at all, explained how they knew that this addition to their family would be more than happy to keep his room clean. They explained how they were more than willing to teach him everything he needed to know about keeping a clean room and a clean house. They did say something about Johnny's age, but added that one is never too young to learn.

After the social worker left, Johnny lay on his new bed wondering what he was to do next. His new mother, although he would never call her that, called him down for a bit of lunch. The man of the house was home, because he had taken the day off. He was sitting at the table eating some sandwich and drinking something from a glass full of ice. As Johnny sat down, The lady gave him a peanut butter and jelly sandwich, telling him he was also going to have milk. She said that he was to finish everything and he must be careful. Spills were not tolerated and, well, he needed to just not make a mess. She also told him that they wanted to teach him the proper way to live in their house, or there would be consequences.

Johnny learned what that meant the hard way. When he would make a mess or say something the family didn't approve of, he was disciplined. If he didn't clean up after himself, he was disciplined. If he didn't make his bed, in the morning, he was disciplined. And that discipline always came in the form of a spanking. If the man had been drinking, he became even more angry and if Johnny did something the foster parents really hated, he would get a longer spanking with the man's big hands. It was not one that would leave red streaked blisters, but it was one that was enough to hurt like the dickens and Johnny would cry for quite a while.

The smell of booze quickly taught Johnny how to create a defense mechanism for his safety. Even at the early age of four, he found out that if he could make others laugh, or even smile a bit, the beatings didn't last as long. His actions and quick-witted expressions, along with the effects of alcohol on the adults, brought somewhat of a smile to them. Sometimes he would cross his eyes and make a funny face. Sometimes he would just plead like he was kneeling in prayer. He learned what made the adults tick;

he learned what would make them less aggressive. Somehow, he could warm them up just enough to get less of a spanking, which was the only thing he wanted. He would make stupid sounds or repeat a nursery rhyme he had heard before. Adults didn't hit hard when they heard a four-year-old try to say something like twinkle twinkle little star, especially when he couldn't properly say the letters w and s. It would come out as tinkle tinkle lil tar. Another thing that would ease the disciplined was simply saying things like a cow goes to the moo vies! Many times, that was all it took to stop his foster father. After all, it was he who dished out most of the punishment, although the foster mom did nothing to stop it. Johnny did whatever it took. It was almost as if he were manipulating them a bit. It wasn't an evil thing; it was a coping thing and it was necessity for his young survival.

There were times when Johnny did something wrong and maybe it was deserving of punishment. He knew he was about to be physically treated in a less than desirable way. Sometimes, though, the assaults came for no reason at all or at least for something he didn't do on purpose. One time he was eating dinner and his arms flew apart as they hit and broke a dish. It was an accident and he tried to tell everyone that it was just an old dish anyway. Johnny slumped in his chair when he saw his foster father raise his hand in the air. He knew he could run, but he also knew he couldn't hide.

Johnny did learn a lesson that he wished he didn't have to learn, It was called being a tattletale. There was one horrible time when his foster father found out that Johnny had been talking to his social worker about how he didn't like the spankings he got. After explaining to the social worker that he and his wife never beat children, he expressed that Johnny was probably making it all up for attention, because that's what foster kids always did. Johnny's foster father decided to teach him a lesson. The lesson was a painful one, but Johnny got the message. No one discussed family problems to someone else outside the family.

Each beating made Johnny more bitter inside. They hurt, and at first, he screamed and cried. All Johnny was ever told was that if he kept screaming, he would get more. Eventually, the screams and cries turned to only cries and then to just sobbing. He had learned the beatings didn't last as long when he didn't scream and just took it. After the spanking, he cried a little, but then he would go to his room, jump on his bed, and day dream about some happy family where love was the center of the relationship.

It was a great dream and a wonderful pretend family. The mother hugged the father, the father patted the son on the head, and they spread a blanket on the ground to ate a picnic lunch together. Johnny could almost see a giant maple tree, next to a little pond where his pretend dad could fish away the hours and Johnny could sit next to him and watch. He could dangle his little feet in the water, and that alone would sooth his real pain. A shout usually brought Johnny back to reality. The sounds of the birds singing, the river rushing, and people laughing were soon replaced by screaming, a door slamming, and a person yelling in the other room. The argument ordinarily was about him and how he just wasn't fitting in with their family. Johnny always had a feeling what would follow these types of arguments. He just knew he was about to go to another foster family. After all, he had been told many times that he was not worthy of being a part of a real family. He didn't like change, but getting away from these people would be for the better. He didn't have a say in anything, anyway. Johnny only hoped that wherever he ended up, it might be better on him then where he was now.

Chapter 3

Family Two and The TV

JOHNNY MET HIS SECOND family when he was almost five. He thought that maybe things were going to get better this time. The house he was to live in was larger than the last. It was further from the inner city where he had spent the first five years of his life. This house wasn't connected to any other houses, like the row homes Johnny had lived in before. The outside was white block and it didn't match the colors of other houses on the street. There were blue ones, tan ones and even a yellow painted house on the block where Johnny was to live. There were more trees here than Johnny had ever seen in the inner city and they were bigger, too.

Inside was similar to the last home Johnny was living in. It still had two stories with the living area found on the bottom floor, and the bedrooms occupying the top floor. This living room was bigger than the last and it had more modern furniture than he was used to. These homes were different and not as crowded looking as the row houses Johnny was familiar with. It was certainly a change.

As a matter of fact, Baltimore, itself was changing and beginning to grow. The growth was not for people, though, but for businesses and new highways and roads. Folks were starting to leave the city and move to an area less congested. Houses were being bought by city planners and corporations, torn down, and turned into office buildings and new shopping strip malls. The city was losing five hundred to eight hundred houses a year, so change was always in the air, and this new house and new block proved that to Johnny. Although all of the changes Baltimore was facing didn't directly affect Johnny, it did factor into where he was going to live now.

As Johnny looked around, he thought this move might actually be a good one. New foster parents, new neighborhood, and maybe this family was much nicer than the last. It didn't take a long time to find out that it was going to be a different experience. As a matter of fact, if you had asked Johnny even at this early age, he would say in his experience, things usually went from bad to worse. but at this point, he didn't want to lose hope. After all, Johnny did get to leave the spanking family.

He soon found out, though, that he was jumping from the frying pan into the fire. At first, just as before, everything was wonderful. This new family smiled and told Johnny he was more than welcome. They sat down, Mother and father on the couch next to their own boy, who was younger than Johnny. He appeared to be about three and Johnny was glad that he now had a chance to have a young brother. The social worker, sitting across from them, explained that Johnny was a good boy and didn't cause much trouble. She commented to this new set of parents how Johnny had a hard time of it with the last family.

Johnny stood beside the worker listening to her talking about discipline and how the Service had no idea that this boy had been mistreated and as soon as they found out, they decided to make a change. He knew this was not exactly the truth, because he had complained to the social worker on occasions and nothing had been done until the adults wanted him out of their home.

Johnny began to look around at these new surrounding as he halfway listened to the mother and father speak about how they had found an alternative to spanking and Johnny would never have to worry about a belt beating again. He smiled and continued looking around the room. He stopped his gazing and starred at the box setting in the corner. This box had an ovel screen on the front with an on and off button. There was another button below the first with numbers on it. On the top of the box was a contraption that looked like alien antenna Johnny had seen on comic books taken from him at his last home. He knew what it was, but he was hardly ever allowed to watch TV at his first foster home. This new mother saw him and asked if he liked watching cartoons on television. Johnny's smile widened and he nodded, thinking that was the right thing to do. He remembered, then, why he had never been allowed much television before. It was because he had been told on many occasions that he didn't deserve it.

His smile soon turned downward a bit, as he listened to an explanation of how watching television was a privilege and good actions brought about good reactions. Johnny knew what that meant. He wondered how many times his actions, whether they were his fault or not, would cause him to lose the privilege of this television. He did try to tell himself he could do what was expected of him. He imagined only the best outcome and if he tried really hard, he would earn a spot in front of that T.V. Watching cartoons, westerns, and, if he were really good, he could join the Mickey Mouse Club.

Johnny began to settle in. At first everything was polite. The adults allowed Johnny to watch TV. It was a well-known secret that adults could do anything they wanted as long as the television babysat the kids. This family was no different. The more TV Johnny watched the more time there was for the mother figure to pay attention to her own child. Almost all attention was given to her natural born, and although Johnny knew it, he didn't care because he had "Mighty Mouse" and "Roy Rogers" to bring a smile to his face and it was so much easier to hide fear and pain when a kid had cartoon friends.

Problems began, though, when Johnny started getting blamed, not only for things he did, but for things he didn't do. There was one time when a plant had been knocked over while he and his foster brother were playing in the same room and Johnny, of course, received the blame. Once he was punished because toys had been left on the floor. He knew that he hadn't left them there, because he really didn't have any toys of his own. These parents told Johnny how terrible he was for taking their child's toys, playing with them, and then leaving them in the way, so that someone was bound to trip over it. When something like this would happen, Johnny would be shoved into a corner and made to stand there listening to why he was useless and why no one really wanted him. The foster parents were right about one thing. There were never beatings. The punishment he did receive and the way he had been talked to, however, in many ways hurt more than the beatings.

There were everyday ups and downs. Sometimes everything went smoothly and all four of them would enjoy the company of each other, but this was rare. There was always an impression of something being wrong that seemed to constantly be in Johnny's head. Maybe he was the one putting it there, or maybe there really was a division of feelings between natural family and the little foster boy. No matter how hard he tried, Johnny could just sense that he didn't entirely belong.

If something is repeated long enough it will be believed, even if it isn't true. Johnny was no different than anyone else when it came to this. Being called useless became as painful as the beatings to him and it wasn't long before he became convinced that what he had constantly been told, was true. If something did go wrong, Johnny could be heard saying that he was never good at anything anyway. Although there was no spanking, the mental beatings started to affect Johnny. He stopped smiling and stopped listening. He was told to do something, and he would refuse, choosing to stand in a corner rather than choosing to do chores. There were even times he would wake early and turn on the television as soft as it would go, watching without permission.

For a while, this worked. He could watch a cartoon or two and turn it off when he heard another family member stirring. He would make it back to his room before anyone noticed. There was a problem, though. In the fifties, televisions were made of a thing called vacuum tubes and tubes got hot. They were slow to cool when turned off, but Johnny had never noticed this, so he felt he was getting away with something.

Sometimes, horrible things follow horrible ideas. One morning, everyone else was still asleep and Johnny decided he would watch some cartoons before anyone got up. He went into the living room, not even getting dressed, just in case he had to make a speedy escape to his bedroom. He was quiet and made sure the volume would not be loud enough to wake anyone. He began watching his favorite show because he loved the star, Buffalo Bob and his puppet Howdy Doody. He watched as Buffalo Bob and a character named Clarabell the clown, went to France. They were looking for another character named Cornelius Cobb who was called Corny.

As Johnny watched, silently as he could, he heard the shuffle of little feet. His foster parents' little son apparently was not asleep and, for a three-year-old, had a great set of lungs. He began singing the theme song of the show and Johnny tried to shush him. Johnny felt that the three-year-old always seemed to want to get him into trouble. When he heard Johnny trying to silence him, he made sure he was loud enough to wake his mom and dad singing over and over, "It's Howdy Doody time, It's Howdy Doody time, Bob Smith and Howdy Doo, Say Howdy Doo to you."

The adults woke up, and when they came into the room, Johnny had turned off the TV and was sitting quietly on the couch. It didn't take long for the foster parents to figure Johnny had been watching TV. They simply touched the top and felt the heat still coming from the set. Johnny looked away as he was asked a barrage of questions about how long this had been going on and about how he could dare break rules set for their family. As the foster father took his hands off the heat coming from the vacuum tubes inside the set, Johnny got that feeling in his gut that made him sometimes want to curl up and hide from the world. He didn't even try to argue when they blamed him for not only waking up their child, but for causing a ruckus on a day where they could have slept in.

Pain came in different forms for Johnny. He had figured out abuse was abuse whether it was caused by a spank or some other form of punishment and he was used to just about every form. When he was punished this time, however, it was something even he didn't expect. His foster father grabbed him by the arm and led him to the back porch door. He opened the door, and with one swift motion, threw Johnny out onto the porch, shut the door, and locked it. It wouldn't have been so bad if it hadn't been the beginning of October and a coldish late fall day. To add insult to injury,

Johnny was still dressed in his underwear. He was getting colder by the minute and he was more embarrassed than he had ever been in his life.

It was, to Johnny, what seemed to be an eternity before his foster mother opened the back door and asked him if he had learned a lesson. Johnny shook his head, but said nothing as he came in wiping what felt like frozen tears from his eyes. He was sent straight to his bed, and he curled up, under the sheets shutting out everything. Once again, he wished himself into a world where he had his own mother and father, where they showed him love, and where he imagined nothing but peace and joy surrounding him.

Johnny figured he was not long for this home, either. After the television episode, he could tell the foster parents didn't want him. No one wanted him. For the remaining few months, he spent at this house, he refused to say anything. He didn't take responsibility for the things he had done wrong, and he didn't defend himself when he was blamed for things their child had done. He pretty much crawled inside himself and lived in his pretend world. He was, however, certainly glad when he was given a little gray suitcase, by his social worker, which he used to pack his underwear, three shirts, one extra pair of sneakers, and his two pair of pants. That was all he really owned and it took no time at all to ready himself for his next foster care home.

Chapter 4

The Care-less family, the Bees, and the Bite.

SPRING CAME, AND WITH it a new family. Johnny walked up to his new row house, in his new neighborhood, to meet his new foster parents. The house offered little front yard space since most of the homes simply sat next to the sidewalk and then the road. Each house Johnny viewed, in both directions, was much like the others. The occasional difference could be seen in the front doors because some had been painted in different colors. He did giggle to himself, though, wondering, once again, if someone might have gone to the wrong house for dinner, because they had mistaken another home for their own.

Johnny and the social worker went into the house and Johnny met the new foster parents. They were a bit older than the last two and said that except for good manners, good behavior, and a willingness to play in the sunshine, they didn't have too many other rules. Johnny seemed to like this man and woman more than any of the others and their home, although neat, was not overly clean. The two adults showed Johnny around and led him to his upstairs bedroom. It was very similar to what he was used to, so Johnny settled right in.

In the weeks and months that followed, he was pretty much left to himself, because the adults, too, seemed to live in their own little world. They were kind and they were caring, but were much quieter than anyone Johnny had ever met. His new foster mother would read a lot, especially when his foster father went to work. Johnny had no idea what he did, for he, too, never talked much. He would come home from work, sit in his chair smoking his pipe, and ask his wife and Johnny how their day had been. He would read the Baltimore Sun paper and would arguing out load about some opinion page article written by people who didn't like change. One thing that upset him more than anything else was what he called the ignorance of his generation, and he told Johnny he should grow up differently and embrace change, because it would come not matter what. Any other time, Johnny's foster dad was content to rest, eat dinner, listen to his radio, and then go to bed.

Johnny liked the fact that he was allowed to go outside to play in their back yard. Right beyond that, next to the chain link fence, was the back alley where he sometimes heard children playing together. Since this older set of foster parents had said they encouraged outside play where kids could meet other kids and just enjoy the fresh spring air, Johnny went out as much as he could. He did noticed that the back of this property had a connection to the front of his new row house. Each yard look the same. Everyone had a linked fence and every yard touched the alley in the same way. The only difference he could see was the occasional barking dog running back and forth inside certain fences. As a matter of fact, if it hadn't been for a bent fence post by the gate in his new yard, Johnny might have been confused as to which property was his.

It wasn't long before Johnny met a group of kids, playing kick ball one warm Saturday. He watched as one boy rolled a ball to another. That kid kicked the ball and ran to the telephone pole to his right. He touched the pole just as he was hit by the ball thrown by a third boy. Johnny heard one boy's shout of safe. Another yelled that he was out and that he was full of it. The older boy went to the pole, grabbed the younger by the shirt collar and pulled him off the base. At that moment he wanted to play with this group of boys.

Johnny held onto the gate post, in his backyard, and continued to watch the interactions of this group. It was certainly more fun than being with adults all of the time.

The older boy saw Johnny hanging onto the gate and shouted toward him, asking if he had seen the play. Johnny didn't know whether the boy on first was safe, but he knew he wasn't about to make a bigger boy angry at him. Johnny told him he didn't know much, but he kind of thought he was out by a hair. With that, the older boy smiled and told his friends that this new kid must be pretty smart. He turned to Johnny and asked him if he wanted to play.

He said something about Johnny being young, but he had a good eye and that was one thing any team needed. Johnny said that he would, and the older boy told him that he could be the umpire. Johnny didn't care what that was. He didn't even know what he was supposed to do, but he did know enough to simply agree with the older and stronger boy. An actual smile crossed Johnny's face and for the first time in a long time, he actually felt as if he were a part of something and that felt good.

Johnny's involvement with this gang of boys continued every evening and every weekend. It wasn't an actual "gang," but all the boys had fun together and it was a "comradery" sort of thing where all of the boys felt the brotherhood. It didn't matter if they were hitting sticks against the back yard fences, or having a game of pitch and catch with a baseball, or dodge ball, or even a football.

Sometimes, as Johnny played, he could see his foster mother smile as she hung the weekly wash on the backyard clothes line. She enjoyed the fact that she had convinced Johnny to meet and play with others. She had, after all, told him many times that it was simply a way one should grow up and Johnny couldn't agree more because he had never known so much fun could be had.

There were two events about to happen, however, that would place a lasting fear in Johnny. The first came one summer's evening, around dusk. The guys had finished a game of ball and were getting ready to go in for supper. One of Johnny's friends saw a giant hornet's nest attached to a neighbor's back yard shed. Dares began to fly furiously. One boy would dare another to knock it down with a stick or a rock. In turn, boy after boy would say there was no way that he would do it. Then, the oldest, finally double dared Johnny to get as close as he could to the nest, and hit it with a good-sized rock to try to knock it off the building.

Johnny couldn't say no. That would be against the rules of fair play. After all, he had been double dared, and when one was double-dared, there was no way to get out of it. Johnny picked up a good-sized rock and eyed the nest. He took careful aim and let the rock fly. Johnny had no idea that his aim was going to be so good. The rock hit, the nest fell, the hornets began to attack and all of the boys ran in every direction. By the time Johnny got to his back door, he had been stung multiple times.

His foster mom took one look at him and made him lay on the couch. Johnny heard her anxious voice talking to the doctor. He heard her explain how his face was red and swollen to the point of causing his eyes to almost close and how Johnny was going to be the death of her yet. The stings hurt Johnny, and the trip to the doctors was anything but comfortable. The doctor took one look at him and told his foster parents that Johnny would probably be fine, but it would be better if he were given shot of Epinephrine which was used for patients with severe allergies to bee stings. The shot Johnny received would take down the swelling and, in a few days, he began feeling like new. The fear of bees, wasps, and hornets however would not go away. Johnny promised his foster parents that he would never go near a bee's nest again and he thought to himself how he would have no problem keeping his promise.

Hornets were not the only thing that caused Johnny to seek medical attention and they were not the only thing that would give him a lasting fear of something. On one summer weekend, Johnny was walking down his back alley, tapping a stick against his neighbor's fence. As he walked, the even tempo sound made by the piece of wood against metal took Johnny to his favorite pond and field. In his mind, he could see his "imaginary real Family" and they were having a swim together in the pond found on their property. He, along with a real mom and dad would race from one side of the pond to the other. In the middle of the pond, Johnny would stand on his real dad's shoulders and dive off into the warm water. Johnny knew that this had to happen to him one day and he would never give up hoping.

The warm sun, the warm water, and the feeling of love's warmth was lost as his stick got caught on a chain link and flipped over the fence, landing just out of his reach on the other side. Johnny looked around, saw his stick and decided to retrieve it. A quick climb over the fence and he could get back to his rhythmic play. He could once again be dreaming of all the fun he would experience with a real set of parents.

As Johnny jumped over the fence, he grabbed his stick and held it over his head as if he were a triumphant gladiator. He was so involved in his victory, he didn't see the rather large dog running toward him from the side of the house. As Johnny turned, stick still in the air, the dog attacked. As its teeth sank into Johnny's arm; he fell to the ground hitting the dog with the stick. That made the dog release his arm, be it then attacked Johnny's leg biting and snarling as if Johnny were some kind of prey.

Screams brought most of the neighbors to their back doors. Johnny's friends ran to the fence to try to give as much comfort as they could, while the dog's owner pulled their pet off of Johnny and put it inside. Johnny was immediately taken to his foster parents who hurriedly took him to the hospital. Johnny didn't remember the ride to the hospital, but he would never forget the needles and the stitches. It was the first time he had become totally aware of the fact that the loss of blood was directly tied to pain and this was a pain that lasted for quite some time.

His foster mom did try to comfort him and stood by him as the doctor took care of him. But she seemed a little more distant than she had ever been. Johnny herd her tell his foster father that she didn't know how much more of this kind of action and behavior she could take. This naturally added to Johnny's pain, because he began to feel, once again, that foster kids were not real family and they would never be treated like they belonged. When he was stitched up, the doctor gave his foster mom and dad a prescription that would ease the pain and prevent infection. He explained to johnny and his family how he was to keep the wounds clean and how he was going to have to rest for quite a few days so that he could heal and avoid infection.

When Johnny returned home, the reminders of the attack were many. His shirt was not only torn, it was red with blood. The stitches were still painful and every time he thought of the dog, he almost began to cry. His foster parents didn't make things easier either. They complained to Johnny about his behavior and his obvious lack of attention. They blamed him for ruining their afternoon, they blamed him for changing their evening plans, and they blamed him for disturbing the entire neighborhood. Johnny knew that wounds heal, but somehow the inside wounds would hold on much longer than those on his skin. Johnny knew that these parents were older than others, but he didn't understand how they would blame him for what had happened. They had been so nice in the past, and now things were changing and Johnny was so confused.

Eventually, the stitches were removed. The cuts were replaced with new skin, and there was surprisingly little scarring. However, the almost near panic Johnny felt, when he saw any dog coming toward him, or the new fear he had when a bee or hornet flew by, would not go away. He had to face the fact that there were two things he would never bother again. If a bee or a dog ever crossed his path, he decided he would go in the opposite direction, no matter where he was.

Johnny didn't really connect the facts that were occurring during the next few months. His social worker began making weekly visits and, although she would take him to the local deli for lunch, he just didn't understand. Finally she explained that he would be placed into another home. She made sure that he knew it wasn't his fault. It was just that older foster parents sometimes get too sick to care properly for a child. Even though she swore that this move wasn't his fault, Johnny somehow felt he had to be somewhat responsible.

Chapter 5

Family Four and the Unthinkable

JOHNNY GUESSED HE WAS just too much trouble for the older couple with whom he had been living. His social worker had come and explained that a move was necessary because of health issues that had developed with his older foster care parents. She tried to assure Johnny that none of this was his fault. Something things happen and change is inevitable. He slowly packed his little gray suitcase and walked down the stairs. The older couple were there and they genuinely seemed a bit sad, too. For the first time ever, Johnny got a hug on his way out of a home. The couple told him they were sorry, they would miss Johnny and think of him often, and they wished him well. Maybe the social worker was telling the truth. It wasn't really any one's fault that Johnny had to go. It was just one of those things that seemed to happen in Johnny's misunderstood world.

Soon, Johnny would find himself being presented to yet another family; they were a man and woman who also swore they had all the love in the world to give to a now seven-year-old boy. As Johnny was sitting in the back seat of the social workers car; he watched row house after row house as they passed by. He did see something interesting, which he had never observed before Looking out the window a rather large tower appeared behind the row houses. It seemed to Johnny to almost touch the clouds.

The social worker interrupted his thoughts and told him they were close to his new home, Johnny then asked about the giant tower he had seen. The social worker explained that what he saw was the tower for WJZ television. She started talking about how she loved that station, especially the Buddy Deane Show which was a dance program like American Bandstand. Johnny had no idea what she was talking about, but he pretended to be interested. Soon, the car stopped and Johnny realized they had arrived at his new home.

When Johnny walked into this home, which to him was not much different than his old one, he saw his new family. They were friendly looking and smiling from ear to ear and their own children were smiling, too. Johnny couldn't help but wonder if the smiles were as fake as the family could be. For a seven-year-old, Johnny seemed to have an extra amount of doubt and much less trust when it came to what was being shown to him. After all, his entire life, so far, had revealed to him nothing to prove anything differently.

Johnny was introduced to each family member. The mother was a very pretty woman, but a bit thin, according to Johnny. She had reddish hair down to her neck and she was dressed in a light blue blouse with a dark blue skirt that came down just passed her knees. Anyone could tell she was fashion conscious, and was totally different than her husband. He was in blue jeans, which had large cuffs, and a turtleneck sweater which appeared to have some stains in the front and sides. Johnny just imagined that if something had been spilled near him, this man used his shirt to clean it up.

Next Johnny was introduced to the children. The girl was about three and she smiled a little smile, but said nothing and acted as if she were a bit shy. The boy was closer to Johnny's age and said it would be good if the two of them could play. Johnny agreed, but thought about his past interactions, or lack of them, especially when it came to a family who had not one, but two natural children. Johnny did, however, hold out hope this time that the two of them could, indeed, play well together.

As he was shown around the place Johnny ended up in a room on the second floor. This bedroom had two dressers, on each side of the room. A bunk bed was positioned next to the window and Johnny saw the top bunk sheets and blanket were tossed around. It was then he was told that one other child was involved in this family, but he, like Johnny, was a foster child. He was a much older boy, who had trouble with pretty much everything. The oldest foster son wanted to create havoc and pretty much get his own way. Unfortunately, for Johnny, the only bed for him was the bottom of the bunkbed in the room he would have to share with the older boy.

At first, everything was almost perfect. Johnny, pretty much, was accepted by the family.The child closest to his age shared his toys, played with a modest bit of fairness, and was always out to have fun. Johnny went to school, and did what normal boys did. He wasn't very good at his work: math was hard, English gave him a headache, and reading was the worst. Johnny didn't know whether it was because he was dumb, or maybe it was just because he didn't care, Whatever it was, he put in the hours, only so he could stay out of trouble and eventually get to the important things—playing.

At home, he was allowed to share his ideas and his feelings and he was recognized as if he were really a natural part of the family. For the first time, he felt like he was a part of a household. He was able to share the toys owned by the other children, because there was an understanding that the rule of the house was "share and share alike."

Fighting wasn't allowed and punishment was confined to what was called "time out" which made Johnny feel much less fearful of adults and older people, except for the older foster kid. Johnny didn't have much interaction with him. The kid didn't speak much and kept to himself quite a bit. When night time came, Johnny was usually asleep when this older boy entered into the room. A few times Johnny would hear him climb to the top bunk and make strange noises and grunts as he was trying to sleep.

Just as Johnny was becoming comfortable with his surroundings, and just as he was beginning to trust others, the worst thing he could ever imagine began to happen. The other family members started to notice that Johnny withdrew from family play. He didn't speak much, and he did little to share any ideas and feelings with the rest of the family. The foster parents tried to ask Johnny what was going on, but all they would hear, as an answer, was the word nothing. Johnny stayed to himself, spending hours in his room, until his older brother walked in. It was then that Johnny would go to the living room and sit on the floor, staring at nothing until it was time to go to bed. For the first time ever, he acted as he didn't want to go to his room to sleep, saying that he wasn't tired and he would like to stay up. Other than that, he said nothing.

In the late fifties and early sixties, somethings were never discussed. As a matter of fact, Johnny well knew that one never shared the family's dirty laundry outside the house. The worst thing that could happen to a child would happen - if someone outside the home found out a nasty secret about any member of any family. Johnny didn't know what this "worse" thing could be, but he wasn't about to find out. What was happening to him was never going to get out.

The embarrassment alone would be devastating. He could never speak of the bruises he had received from his older foster brother. He could never talk to anyone about the nights he was awakened, from a deep sleep, just to have his foster brother smack him around, punch him repeatedly, and do whatever he wanted to a defenseless child. After all, Johnny knew if he had opened his mouth he would get even more beatings and receive much more painful indignities. Johnny had nowhere to turn and no one to talk to. Even worse, he didn't think he could talk to anyone about what was going on, anyway. Johnny remained silent with this secret. He shoved it so far into his subconscious as he could; he would purposely not remember the things happening to him anyway, even he wanted to.

He never ever spoke about the things that had gone on until one sad day when he went to the doctors for his yearly check-up.

While at the doctor 's office, the nurse noticed the black and blue marks on both the front and back of his legs, on his upper arms, and on his back. Because of the fact that he was part of the foster care system, the nurse felt it was her duty to report this to social services. As far as Johnny knew, there was no law requiring her to make the call because child abuse policies were in their infancy. She was someone, however, who genuinely cared for others, especially children. One phone call let the social worker know that something was apparently happening.

When she met Johnny the next day, she tried to get him to talk about the bruises. Johnny stared straight ahead and didn't say anything. She told him he had to say something, or there was nothing she could do to stop whatever was going on. She tried over and over again to make Johnny tell her, but he remained silent. She explained that no matter what it was she could help and she placed her hand gently on Johnny's shoulder, Johnny pulled away and sat there quietly. Inside, he knew she could not help. He was being pulled apart, but on the outside, he refused to show any emotion, display any fear, or share any words except, "I just fall a lot, and sometimes I get hurt in baseball. That's all." After that silence was all he would do. The foster care worker couldn't get anything out of the family, and, as far as they knew, Johnny was a clumsy. They had no other ideas. Everyone knew something was wrong and change was needed.

It wasn't long before Johnny was heading to yet another home. Maybe it was a request from the parents or maybe it was just a way to keep him a bit safer. No matter the cause for the decision, Johnny was glad, but he was sad too because he was on his way to home number five. He was only seven, but the world had almost convinced him he was worthless and unlucky when it came to love or being a part of anything. He could not comprehend the fact that none of this had been of his own doing. He began to let hate take over. He hated adults. He hated kids, especially those who had a real family, and he was beginning to hate his own life. Most of all, he hated the foster care world.

For a moment, though, he imagined he was standing in a room that was his. He looked around and saw a single bed . . . his bed. He heard noises from the other room. To him it was a real mom singing as she did house work. He could almost smell the aroma of a pipe that he imagined his real dad enjoyed as he read the evening paper. This was a world where he could be happy and he would feel real love. It was a love that had gone from him when he first left his natural mom and dad.

A voice calling out silenced his dream and he crossed the room to his dresser. Johnny stood silently as he emptied out that dresser. He slammed his belongings into his gray suitcase and took one last look at the room that he had grown to hate. He walked slowly down the stairs to meet the awaiting social worker. As he went out the door, he glanced back at the family who had probably been the first to show the most positive feelings for Johnny. He got into the back seat of the social worker's car and waited silently.

Chapter 6

Bad Paint

THERE WASN'T MUCH MEMORABLE about family five, except for the fact that the house was old and musty. Johnny thought the couple who had accepted him into their home were a bit musty, too.He didn't mind that they were older, but to him they smelled like the house. The woman was chubby and looked like she enjoyed a good large supper on more than one occasion. She was a happy sort of a woman, though, who reminded Johnny of a picture he had once seen of an older maid on the cover of one of the Saturday Evening Posts. The man of the house, too, was older. He wore overalls and a red plaid shirt which always smelled like cigarettes. They both had gray hair, but his was thinning and her hair was up in a bun.

Everyone sat in the living room, with the social worker explaining a bit of Johnny's past. Johnny looked around the room as they talked. The couch, where the foster parents sat, was almost pink in color. In front of it was a dark brown table that appeared to have handles on either side of it, but it was a bit dusty. The chair, where Johnny sat was a high back chair which was designed with pink flowers. There was a desk, too, with a wooden chair which had a black and white cushion on the seat. The curtains were striped, but they didn't match the furniture which, in turn, didn't match the floor rugs. Johnny didn't care though about the furniture. As he finally listened to what was being said, he heard the adults assuring him that everything was going to be fine.

When they had all finished talking, the couple led Johnny to his new room. It looked comfortable enough, although no one could convince him this was a more permanent move for him. He would not allow himself to get too comfortable in a place he was sure was just limited stay for him. As Johnny looked out his new room's windows, he saw the tiny back yard of his new home. It would have been a more beautiful view, if there had been anything there except for a brick wall belonging to the house across the alley.

The windows were dirty and the wood around them were painted a dark green. The walls of his room were a lighter green than the windows, but both were pealing and cracked paint was lying all over. Johnny imagined it had not been touched up in years. A moldy scent came from the window sill, but when opened, the city air masked the smells of the room. That sill, however, was Johnny's favorite place to sit. He would look out and down, and dream of a better life that had to be waiting for him, and his thoughts kept telling him that there must be a better life somewhere—anywhere but in the city.

His dream family was waiting for him—he just knew it. They were ready to take him in and share their life with him. He could imagine the fun times they would all have during the spring and summer, sitting outside and enjoying a glass of lemonade. Johnny would see, in his mind, the nights they would sit around the table playing games, reading funny stories, and sometimes watching TV together. As they watched they would share a bowl of popcorn. He could just taste the butter filled treat.

The illusion left him quickly as he realized he was actually chewing on some of the paint chips that were on the window sill. He felt a bit stupid when he understood that his dream was causing him to do something without even realizing it. Reality also brought thoughts of loneliness and a feeling of being unwanted. Deep inside Johnny's heart was aching and he felt hopeless.

Days wore into weeks and weeks into months. Johnny went to school, came home to a lady that told him to go to his room and do his homework, assuming he had homework. He would go to his room and sit on the sill. Homework wasn't important to Johnny and he knew that no one would be checking behind him, anyway. As a matter of fact, he wasn't even sure the lady knew much of anything about crafts, adding and subtracting, or writing. She was kind, yes, but she had no answers for the question Johnny had asked concerning something he may had tried to learn at school. If it had to do with math, or writing she always told Johnny to look in his book and she was sure he could find the answer in there.

The one thing she did know how to do was cooking. Every dinner was good and cooked to perfection. Johnny guessed that is why neither one of the adults looked like they had missed a meal. At dinner, he would come to the table, swear he had completed his homework, and eat what he always considered a wonderful meal. To him, it didn't matter whether it was a plate full of spaghetti, or a bowl of re-warmed stew, the taste was pretty mouthwatering.

After dinner, he would sit with his foster parents and listen to the radio. They loved classical and jazz, so they listened to this new station WHFS. They tried to explain to Johnny how this was the first FM stereo station in the Baltimore and Washington area and they were lucky to get it. Johnny could not have cared less. There was no television and Johnny hated reading, so he half-heartedly listened to the band music and the mundane voice of the announcer. When it was bed time, he was told once to go, and he tucked himself in, falling asleep to the night sounds of the city that had become a routine part of life - not a good life, but his life.

In the fifties and sixties, material things didn't have the same stringent requirements they would have in future years. Government regulations didn't concern themselves, for example, with toys made of unknown materials. Some of the biggest sellers of toys were made from dangerous substances such as lead. City water, too, contributed to elevated levels of lead in the blood of children. The most common house-hold items found to contain lead, however, was house paint. Little was known, by the average family, about the effects of lead accidentally ingested. As a matter of fact the center for disease control didn't even establish acceptable blood lead levels for kids until the sixties.

Of course, none of this was even known to Johnny or his family. Johnny didn't own any lead army soldiers and the few things he owned had never bothered him. Lead poisoning, though, can be hard to identify. Kids in the sixties, who seemed very healthy sometimes had high levels of lead in their veins. Symptoms of poisoning usually don't show up until dangerous amounts have shown up in the blood.

It wasn't until Johnny began to lose his appetite that his foster parents took notice. It wasn't like Johnny to refuse his foster mother's cooking. One day, he began to physically shake and started to throw up. He had a very high fever, and that was when his foster family decided a doctor's care was in order. Both foster parents piled into the family station wagon and drove to the doctor's office as Johnny sat in the back seat feeling worse than he had ever felt in his life.

The doctor's visit only caused the fear in Johnny to increase. He certainly didn't know why he felt so sick; he knew he hadn't been around anyone else who had a flu or severe cold. After a cursory exam, the doctor suggested that the family take their foster boy to the hospital for some tests. They asked what he thought was wrong with Johnny, but all the doctor would say was he didn't have the equipment to make any further diagnosis.

When they arrived at the Maryland Medical Center, Johnny went into the emergency room. The nurses put a blood pressure cup on his arm and put a thermometer under his tongue. They were so nice, speaking in such mild tones and sweet voices, that the blood pressure and temperature were a breeze for Johnny. When the doctor came in, he began asking one question after another. Johnny, nor his foster mom and dad, had answers to give the doctor. He began an examination and it was only when the doctor ordered blood tests, that Johnny started to well up with tears mixing with sweat.

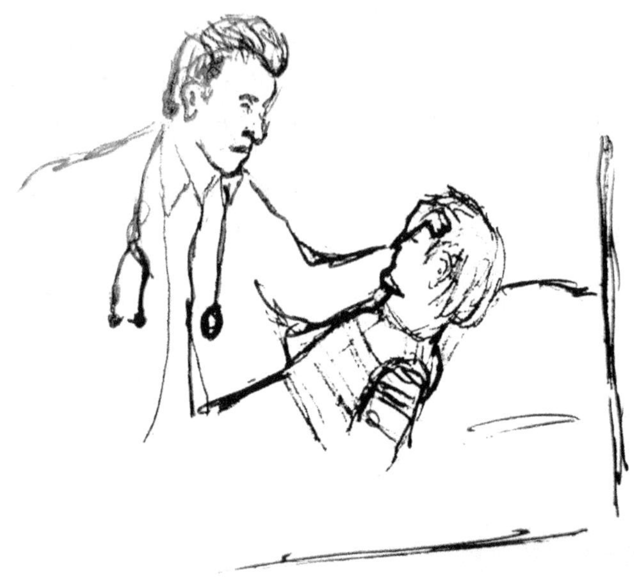

When the nurse came in with a series of needles and tubes, Johnny began to cry out with fear. His foster mom sat with him explaining that everything was going to be fine. She held his hand and rubbed his forehead, stroking his hair to calm him down. Calmness, though, didn't come back until the blood had been drawn, and the nurse had told Johnny that she was finished.

Johnny didn't know it, but he was far from finished. He had never been through something like this and he had no idea what was really going on. An orderly came in next and told all of them that the doctor had ordered some x-rays. He took Johnny to the radiation department, talking to him all the way. Johnny's foster mom walked along his side still holding his hand. The orderly explained that they were going to take special pictures of Johnny's inside. Because Johnny was obviously afraid, the orderly added that this didn't hurt one bid and would be over in a jiffy.

When the X-rays had been taken, Johnny went back with his mom and the orderly. The doctor was there and began talking to

Johnny's foster parents. He couldn't understand why the Doctor was not talking to him as well, but he really knew that children were always the last to know what was happening. It was only after Johnny heard that he was to be given a special medicines that he found out he had lead poisoning.

He heard the doctor tell his foster parents that he had a lead level that was way too high. He explained how Johnny had gone through a complete head-to-toe physical to look for signs of any organ damage, and chelation therapy should be initiated. He tried to listen to the conversation, but only heard a few words, like charcoal and chelation therapy, whatever that was, and something called EDTA. He was filled with fear, when he found out that the medicine would have to go into his arm, but was a bit comforted by the same nurse that had taken his blood for testing.

With all the words he had heard and all the procedures he was going through bouncing around his thoughts and some kind of medicine going through his body, he began to rest a little. Johnny found, too, that he was going to be staying in the hospital for a while, and would have to be monitored. He overheard that he might need a second course of chelation therapy. Eventually, though, time led to sleep and that was the best thing Johnny could do.

Johnny got better and was going to be released from the hospital. His folks had been given information about lead paint and his foster dad had repainted Johnny's room while his foster mom was spending time with Johnny. She also told johnny that his foster dad would have the entire house painted, soon, so there was no chance he would get sick again.

Johnny's foster parents seemed to change when they got home from the hospital. They paid more attention to him, and somehow their food even tasted better to Johnny than he had remembered. The biggest surprise, when he got home, was the brand-new television which he was allowed to watch. He couldn't believe his luck had changed for the better. Johnny loved shows like "Father Knows Best" and "My Three Sons," but his favorite show was "The Lone

Ranger." In his mind he, too, was an unknown cowboy, a Texas Ranger, who would come riding in just in time to save the day.

Johnny finally thought that maybe things were beginning to improve for him. He was being visited by the social worker on a more frequent basis, and spent a quite a bit of time at the Department of Social Services. What he didn't know was that a couple who lived in a place called Sandymount, a quiet little community in the country, were interested in adopting him.

Chapter 7

The Final Foster Family

MIRACLES HAVE BEEN OCCURRING for thousands of years and many people just refuse to believe that the possibility exists. Johnny, for the first time in his life, wanted to believe in miracles. It was in November of 1961 that Johnny was about to find out a true blessing was to become a reality. He was visited by the social worker, which usually meant he was about to change families or there was a problem that had occurred. Because of the way his foster parents had changed, they included Johnny in everything that they planned. Being with them had become more of a joy than any other home in which he had lived. He didn't understand why he was possibly being moved.

This visit was a mixture of emotions. Johnny could not believe how much of a roller coaster ride his existence had become. This time, though, the social worker was there to give Johnny some very good news. Johnny wasn't too sure. He didn't understand why he couldn't stay with the parents where he was currently living. The social worker informed Johnny that he was going into what was called a transition foster home.

She explained how this was a family who really cared about all children and they would help Johnny adjust to a more permanent situation. She emphasized the fact that these foster parents had specialized training and were successful with kids in transition. She also explained how this couple took care of all types of children, but specialized in children that were about to be adopted. It was then that she told Johnny that a family had seen him at the Department of Social Services and that they had asked if they could meet him and possibly adopt him.

Johnny couldn't believe his ears. After four years and after his soon to be sixth and final foster home, Johnny was about to live in a permanent homee with a real family. It was the first time in these four years that he grinned from ear to ear because he was truly happy. Apparently, the adults he was living with had been told of the move and had known about it for some time. They, of course, were not allowed to tell Johnny, but they were truly happy for this new turn of events. The mom hugged Johnny and said she loved him and would never forget him, but she was so happy for him because he was about to become a real family member of a loving home.

Johnny went to his room with his foster mom and began to pack his things. As he was filling his suitcase, His foster mom handed him a little package. Johnny didn't know whether to cry or shout for joy. He quickly opened the gift and, in his hands was a signed photo of his hero. He stared at the picture of the Lone Ranger standing next to his horse, Silver. His foster mom read the inscription and explained that the picture came from some company named Merita Bread. She had been saving it and she thought this was the perfect time to give it away. After asking Johnny to take good care of the picture, the two hugged and His foster mom kissed him on the forehead. She told Johnny that he would always be her favorite boy.

Johnny carried his little gray suitcase and all his worldly possessions with a bit more of an excited bounce in his step. He had carefully placed his new gift in his suitcase under his clothes, so that it wouldn't tear or bent while moving. He got into the back seat of the social worker's car and waved as they pulled off. He waved to his foster parents, he waved to the house, and he waved to the old neighborhood. He knew this place would always be a good memory for him, even though he had gone through a time of sickness and pain.

Johnny's thoughts then went to possible future events. His daydream consisted of what it would be like living in the country. He wondered what his real parents might be like and act like. He didn't have any idea, but it didn't matter. The social worker had told him that he had been chosen. He was finally wanted just because he was himself.

First, however, he would have to make it through this last foster home. Johnny believed that this would be a breeze; he could coast through this one. Nothing was going to get in the way of his chance to become a real son to a real father and a real mother. He would have coasted, too, if it hadn't been for the very angry and a very jealous older boy he was about to meet.

Johnny was introduced to this new foster family with smiles and hugs. This couple seemed like they were very kind. They were not too old and not too young. They sat Johnny down on the couch and explained to him how he would have to follow all of their rules, and he would also have to be responsible for certain chores. Johnny didn't care. He would do anything necessary that would get him closer to a real family. Johnny agreed that he would do as they said. He would complete his chores and do more if it were needed. He wanted to be prepared for his real family and he knew this would help him adjust.

These transition foster parents showed him their home. Because it was so familiar looking to Johnny, he assumed that maybe all city homes must have been designed by the same people. Every single one he had lived in was so similar that settling in was no problem. Johnny unpacked, and carefully put his clothes in their proper dresser drawers He took special care to place his autographed photo where it would be safe. Then, he returned to the living room to talk to his new parents.

These parents further explained what they expected out of Johnny and how honesty was the one thing they prized over everything else. He was also told how he would soon meet one more family member when that boy returned home because, apparently, he had been visiting a friend. Johnny was also warned that this boy was a bit older, and had been in the foster care system for more than twelve years. Johnny knew what that meant and concluded that he would stay as far away from this boy as possible. After all, he knew this boy may be destined for a life filled with foster homes until he reached the age of eighteen. It was pretty much a given, in the foster program, that a child who had reached the age of fourteen or so was not going to be a part of a permanent family. It was also a given that a child in this situation usually lived with a chip on his or her shoulder. This type of child was not to be trusted and younger foster children stayed as far away as possible.

After the social worker left, Johnny wanted to impress this new set of parents. He asked them if they wanted him to do anything for them, but they explained how there would be plenty of time for that later. Right now, he could stay in the living room and pick out a toy or a puzzle and enjoy play time until lunch was prepared.

As he picked out a puzzle and began to put it together, his new foster mom smiled and began asking him some things he liked to do. It was easy for Johnny to answer this question. He had done it a hundred times before. He looked around the room and, being an observant child, saw an easel and a painting which seemed to still be drying. He figured this new mother had painted it because the subject was of flowers in a vase and he saw those exact flowers and vase sitting on a small table in the corner. Across the room, he saw a bookshelf with all of the books placed neatly in a row. Each shelf had a bookend and each bookend was shaped like some old famous person. The small bookends reminded him of pictures of old people on a card game he had seen once before.

Johnny turned to the lady of the house and explained how he loved to read and he loved to draw, but that he was not too good at either. He smiled when she told him that maybe she could help him with both because she loved those things too. He asked her who the bookends were and she showed him each one. She picked up the first, explaining that it was the likeness of Mark Twain, a famous writer. Then she showed him one of a guy named Charles Dickens. He listened, be his new foster mother understood that he probably wanted to finish the puzzle he was working on. She excused herself and went to fix lunch.

Johnny was very thankful for everything at that point. He felt comfortable and safe until the door opened and a boy of fourteen or fifteen slammed the door behind himself. He was a scruffy sort of a kid who towered over Johnny and folded his arms, staring straight ahead, as the foster mom came out of the kitchen to introduce the two. She informed them as to how she expected them to get along and that she would not put up with any fighting what-so-ever.

She stared at the older child and sternly explained what she had obviously said to him before. Johnny listened as she repeated her clear instructions on getting along. He looked at the boy who simply grunted and slouched on the couch. He didn't know this particular boy, but he knew this type of boy, and that made him uneasy. The older foster boy staying with this family ignored Johnny at first, but that didn't last long.

In the beginning of their time together, this particular boy would do no more than verbally put down Johnny or tell him he was not worth anything. He would tell Johnny that he was going places, in his life. He was going to make something of himself because he wasn't as stupid as Johnny was. He didn't need people and he certainly didn't need to like people. He was a loner, and he, in no uncertain terms asked Johnny not to get in his way, ever.

It didn't take too long for the verbal abuse to turn physical. The older foster child would sneak up and flick the back of Johnny's ear, just to hear him scream. Then he would leave the room as one of the parents entered to see why Johnny had shouted. Johnny would always make up a story because he knew if he told what had really happened, things would get much worse. It didn't seem to matter, though, because things escalated. The flicking of the ears soon turned to the smacking of the back of Johnny's head. He didn't hit hard; he just wanted to prove to Johnny who was boss. He would show his aggression in many different ways, however, all out of the eyesight of the foster parents. Sometimes he would ball up his fist and feign a punch, just to watch Johnny wince.

Nothing was done to actually hurt Johnny, nothing that is, until the older child overheard his foster mother talking about the adoption to which Johnny was looking forward. Johnny had been warned not to talk about his future plans to become a permanent family member, especially when his older foster brother was nearby. His brother might become angry and take it out on Johnny. How true this warning became. It didn't take long before Johnny's older foster brother started getting more physical. The flicking of the ears and the smacking of the head were no longer gentle reminders. They hurt! Apparently, jealousy was a green-eyed monster, as Johnny had heard before, and this older boy was a monster. Johnny told his foster mother and father about what had been going on.

Both of them talked to the older child. Then they reminded Johnny how honesty would have been the right thing to do. He had kept quiet, and they expressed how he should not have done that. Things could have been stopped a long time ago, if he had only been truthful. After asking Him if he had learned from this experience, he agreed to always confide in them. Johnny knew this, however, would make things worse. After all, this older foster boy would always say he wasn't doing a thing and that Johnny was just trying to get him into trouble making up stories. Besides, as he put it, whenever he did something to Johnny, he was just fooling' around.

Time went by too slowly for Johnny, because he was so excited about the adoption. This was only January, and he was going to have to wait until the end of March, or the first part of April. He just couldn't understand why everything that was good took so long to become a reality. Johnny kept wondering to himself how much paperwork was required for someone to adopt a child. He just couldn't fathom why a court and a judge was a necessity. He had already visited the Social Services building, to meet his new parents on several occasions. They were wonderful and he not only got the chance to see them, he got to talk to them. To him, they were the people he had dreamed about whenever he was hurting or being hurt.

Johnny constantly saw his new mom and dad in his mind. His new mother was a little short, compared to her husband. She talked with a quiet voice and smiled the entire time they were visiting. Johnny's new father to be was a tall man. He didn't have much hair on his head, but Johnny didn't care. He had a kind face and, he too, smiled while talking to Johnny. He could not forget the joy he had felt when they actually asked him if he wanted to come and live with them. His answer of "you bet" played itself over and over in his mind. Each day, during the wait, he would recall the visits and he could do nothing but smile to himself. There were only a few months left to wait and then he would be a member of a real family.

Johnny sat in his room and couldn't help but feel excited about what he would soon be experiencing. As he sat and thought about his visits, he knew what he wanted to do. He decided that the one thing he cherished the most would make a great gift to his new father and mother. Johnny went to his dresser and opened it, looking under his clothes for the autographed photo of the Lone Ranger. The bottom of the drawer, however, was empty. He gave a shout of anger and a bit of sadness because he knew exactly what had happened. The older foster brother had obviously taken it.

Johnny ran down the stairs and straight into the living room. The older foster boy was sitting on the couch, but Johnny's foster mother was nowhere in sight. She had been doing laundry and was probably hanging clothes on the line outside. Johnny's foster dad, naturally, was at work, so Johnny went right up to the older kid, said something about him being a thief, and punched him right in the face. Johnny had never done this before, but stealing his photo was the straw that broke the camel's back.

The older child, naturally being stronger, stood up and grabbed Johnny's arm. He shoved Johnny toward the couch and bent his arm backward. He shouted at him about how he had taken it and how he was glad he had. He got a good bit of cash for it, too. He also began screaming about how unfair it was that a little kid like Johnny would find a home before he did. He was the one who had deserved it.

Johnny started crying as the older boy angrily stared into his eyes and told him if he said anything about this, he would find a way to kill him. It was then that the pent-up anger of the older child showed itself as this kid took Johnny's arm and slammed it over the back of the couch. Screams brought the foster mother from the backyard to the living room. The older foster child began shouting that Johnny and he had been playing cops and robbers and Johnny had fallen against the back of the couch and hurt his arm.

Johnny couldn't talk but could see through his tears the eyes of his older foster brother staring a hole through him. The fear of future harm was much stronger than the pain Johnny was experiencing now, so he said nothing. On the way to the hospital, Johnny tried to be brave. He had never quite felt the kind of pain he was going through and he was truly scared to death of his older foster brother. He really believed this boy would see to his threat and try to kill him.

The doctor ordered an x-ray but explained to Johnny's foster mother that he expected the arm had been broken. After the X-ray showed Johnny had a broken arm, he was asked by the doctor how he had come to fall against the furniture. As a cast was being put on his arm, Johnny held in the truth. He explained how they had been playing with his older foster brother and that it was all an accident. The doctor stated to Johnny's foster mother that he was a bit concerned. He had never seen a fall against a couch break a child's arm quite like this, but as long as Johnny would say nothing there was nothing else that could be done. He gave out instructions for the care Johnny would have to take while he was in a cast.

Johnny's foster mother didn't believe this story either, but until Johnny told her the truth about what had really happened, she decided she would keep a more careful eye on everything that went on under her roof. She reported the incident to the social worker, who talked to Johnny. His story, however, never changed. Fears of the threats made by his older foster brother were much more real than anything the social worker or his foster mom could do to him. Johnny remained totally silent. Johnny's foster care mother promised that she would do everything she could to make sure that Johnny would be safe. She just wanted the truth because the story of an accident just didn't add up, but Johnny knew that this was an empty promise.

She could not be by his side day in and day out. He did tell her that there was more to the story, but he couldn't and wouldn't say anything else. The social worker and the foster mother talked, and the two of them decided that Johnny was to be kept away from the older boy as much as possible. They both knew there was a danger for Johnny, but, if Johnny would refuse to talk, nothing more could be done.

They couldn't remove the older foster brother right away; there was no family who would be able to take him in on such a short notice. Johnny would have to spend the rest of his time at this home within earshot of his foster parents. During the day he would be staying near his foster mom and his nights were to be spent sleeping on the couch. As Johnny patiently waited and spent his time basically at the side of his foster mom, weeks passed and eventually, the cast came off.

The arm had healed, but Johnny wasn't sure he had. However, there were only a few days left where Johnny would have to keep looking over his shoulder. He continued to dream of the life that was about to begin. He envisioned the joy of his soon to be family and the life he would be able to experience. Waiting was so hard for little Johnny L. Mitchell.

Chapter 8

A New Home—A New Family

A SUNRISE CAN BE watched and the colors and warmth that it expresses can last a lifetime. Johnny was up before the sun, and he had already folded the blankets that had kept him warm and safe on the couch. He was at the window of the living room watching the sides of the neighbors' houses lighten as the sun began climbing higher and higher. He loved to watch his world wake up and get brighter and brighter, but that morning he was watching, too, for the social worker that was to take him to her office to begin his new life with a real family. His excitement was almost unbearable and his happiness was unequaled. He, a boy who used to think he was useless, was about to be accepted just for being himself. There was no bad situation he had faced in the past, there was no evil foster brother to beat him, abuse him, or break his arm, and there was no longer any foster parent to treat him like a sub-human being. For Johnny, life could never again get as bad as it had been.

As he watched, his foster mom came into the room and said good morning. Johnny jumped, not expecting to hear anyone, for his mind was elsewhere. His foster mom, seeing this, told Johnny that everything was fine. She was going to make breakfast, and his older foster brother wasn't there. He had gone to visit a friend and was going to spend a few days. Johnny, for a second, wondered how the heck he could keep his cool. He just couldn't wipe the smile from his face. His foster mother asked Johnny what he wanted for breakfast and Johnny told her whatever she made was fine with him.

He soon smelled the bacon frying as he continued looking out the window. When breakfast was ready Johnny tore himself from the window so he could eat. He sat down, making sure he thanked his foster mother for the good food. His foster mom talked to him a bit about his new situation, and about how she and her husband would surely miss him. He was about to be with a new family and she wanted to let him know what a privilege it was to help him get ready for this family. Johnny turned and gave her a giant hug. He couldn't talk right then, but she understood. The social worker picked up Johnny and the ride to the Social Service building was filled with chatter. Johnny could not stop asking questions. Where was his new house? What was the country like? Were there things there that he should know about to better prepare him for the trip? What about the family? Johnny rattled question after question and hardly waited for an answer before asking the next.

All he knew was that he was leaving the awful city that had given him four years living with six different families. He could remember the pain and suffering he had endured, but he also thought of the few good times he had. Now, things would be different and he would be a part of something more than a system which, unfortunately, shuffled children around any time it was needed. Johnny understood it had all been done in the name of safety and security for both adults and children.

None of this mattered anymore when they arrived at the Social Security building. Johnny walked up the steps and into the office with his little gray suitcase in hand. He was more than excited when he, once again, met his new mother and father. After a series of documents were signed, and after saying goodbye to the social worker, Johnny left with his new parents. Smiling from ear to ear, he started to get into their car's back seat. This time, he wouldn't mind sitting in the back because there was a different destination awaiting him. His new father, however, asked if Johnny would like to sit up front in between them, so he could see everything. Cloud nine was not enough of a statement to explain his joy.

Johnny sat in the middle of the front seat and reached over so he could hold his mom's hand. Soon, city became suburb, and suburb became country. He watched as row houses turned to individual homes, with small yards. These homes were not connected but had side yards as well. The further he traveled, the further apart the buildings were. He began to view houses build on more land than he had ever seen. There were actually trees that turned into woods and, in turn, became forests. As his dad drove onto a major roadway, houses began to disappear altogether. He, for the first time, saw openness and space, clear land with trees that seemed to disappear over the rolling hills.

Johnny's new dad had told him that they had a few stops to make before going to their new home, but Johnny didn't mind at all. This was a new adventure and he was all for it. His mom told him to look out the windshield and watch for planes landing and taking off from the airport he supposed they were passing. Soon his father turned into the airport entrance and explained they were going to what was called the observation tower - to watch the planes for a while. Johnny saw the words Friendship International and asked his new mom what it said. She read it to him and he considered it a great omen. His mouth was in an opened position as they parked and walked to the tower. He had never seen actual planes and jets taking off and landing before, and he could barely contain his excitement. As he, his mom, and dad watched, Johnny asked if they were going to take one of them, but was told this time they were only there to watch. Johnny's face was pressed against the glass as he saw the flying craft come and go.

When Johnny turned to ask a question of his mother, he saw her talking to a man he had never seen before. He walked to his mom's side as the man was writing into a book that she had handed him. Johnny's curiosity must have been evident, as his mother introduced the two. She told Johnny that this was a famous man who was an astronaut. His name was John Glenn and he had been the first to go into space and travel around the entire world from miles away. She had also asked for his autograph, so Johnny would have it when he grew up. She handed him a book called "Love is a special way of feeling" by a lady named Joan Walsh Anglund and turned to the first page. There it was and it simply said To Mrs. William Price—John Glenn He handed the book back and saw his father heading to the gift shop. There, his new father brought him a toy. Johnny looked at the box and saw that it was a model of Pan Am's newest jet, and Johnny held back tears as he was handed the toy. Actually, it was the first toy gift he could remember ever being given to him and him alone. He held it close to his chest as he continued to watch the excitement around him. He didn't want any of this to end, but soon, he was told it was time to head home. Head home! These two words bounced back and forth in his mind as he walked back to the car holding hands with both his mom and dad. They left the airport, and soon were riding through an area where there were hardly any houses. All Johnny could see were woods, miles and miles of woods - and roads, miles and miles of roads. To him, this was an entirely new world, but it was his new world and he was happy.

Johnny caught himself saying over and over again the words, "Are we there yet?" His mom laughed and his dad smiled at this, for they knew what excitement did to a young child. Each mile brought more anticipation. Each answer of "soon" just led to more excitement. As the car turned off the main road between Baltimore and Westminster, and as they turned into a long gravel lane, Johnny could see a large white cape cod house at the end of the driveway. He saw the front door and two large windows facing the road. A brick porch was on the side of the house and Johnny could see two windows on the second floor. To him, it was the most beautiful sight he had ever seen. His father mother's and father's hand and walked toward his new home.

Chapter 9

The First Day

ARRIVING AT HIS NEW home with a new family was as exciting as it was scary for eight-year-old Johnny L. Mitchell. First, everything was a surprise. The land was open and bigger than any Johnny had ever encountered. The trees were huge and, certainly not like the ones he had known in the city.

There was a garden pruned and containing beds that had been shaped like stars, a moon, circles and ovals. Each was arranged equal distant from a center circle which contained an evergreen. The flower beds were filled with more roses than Johnny had ever seen in his life. Around the outside of the entire garden were mounds of flowers and he had no idea what they were. All he knew was they were big purple, pink, and white. While looking at all the beauty, Johnny did show his apprehension. His new parents walked alongside him, and he smiled as they explained the new scene and how it now belonged to him as well, since he was now a member of the family.

The house was an all-white cape cod. On the front was a stone porch which simply contained two potted plants on either side of the front door. On each side of the porch were giant window panes, the largest windows Johnny had ever seen. On both sides of the house were other porches. One lead to the living room and contained a wicker plant stand and two wicker rockers. The other was encased with lattes work with a blooming trumpet vine, and this one lead to the kitchen. Johnny walked around the house with his new mom and dad and saw a great metal staircase leading to a second story metal porch.

As Johnny took in the expanse of home and land, his mother explained how their family was a bit extended. They lived on the upper floor, and his new Grandmother lived on the bottom. Though they shared almost everything, including meals which his grandmother was more than accustomed to preparing, there would be times where the three of them would live separately. Johnny climbed the metal steps and stood on the porch, looking out onto a parcel of land containing the formal garden and an opened field ending at a hedgerow of trees and brush. His father pointed to the hedgerow and explained how all of the lands from the road in front, to the trees in the back belonged to the family. Johnny gazed and could only compare the size to an entire block of homes he had known in the city.

His new mother, too, was pointing toward the back lot. Johnny listened as she explained how the garden had been tended by his grandmother, and how each plant and flower had a message and a story. She promised to teach him the meaning of each shape and each flower found there. Johnny could hardly believe the sight in front of him. The land was green and yellow, red and blue, and even purple. He had never encountered anything like this. He never even knew such a thing could exist, but here it was and it was now a part of him.

Before Johnny's mom suggested they go in and get settled she gave him a present. It had been sitting on the porch chair and she had been blocking it a bit from Johnny's view because she had wanted it to be a surprise. Johnny looked and sitting there was the cutest stuffed skunk he had ever seen. He picked it up and began hugging it and stated he was going to call it skunky. He held it tightly as the three of them decided to go inside.

Johnny turned the doorknob to the French door, leading to his new home. This was another first for him. He had never seen a door that had been cut into two pieces so that the top could be opened while leaving the bottom closed and locked. As he entered, he stopped to see a bear rug hanging on the entry wall. His eyes opened a bit wider as his father explained to him how that had been a real bear and a gift from one of his family friends. Johnny looked down the small hall to a room containing a couch and a recliner. He walked a bit closer and noticed a dining room table and four chairs on his left. Although it was cluttered with papers, Johnny was still in awe. He walked to the table, also observing a small kitchen, again on his left. He had seen bigger kitchens, but none of them meant anything to him anymore because this was his!

Johnny's mom called him back to the hall and led him to a little bedroom, where he could see a bed, a set of drawers built into a wall under a window, a small desk and chair, and a sliding door leading to a small closet. Looking past the bed and dresser drawers, he could see a window and a view of a great maple tree which seemed to wave welcome in a gentle breeze. Johnny could not believe this was all happening to him.

Previously, thinking his life was destined to be a series of different houses and families, and people who could care less about his wellbeing, Johnny wiped away a tear of joy realizing this was all real. He finally knew he had a family. He had a home. He even had his own room, his own land, his own garden . . . and it was all for keeps. It was better than any of the dream she had come up with during the many times he had faced hardships. This was real!

Johnny thoughts were interrupted by an unknown voice coming from the bottom of the inside steps, which lead to the first floor. The voice sounded happy and warm. It was his grandmother and she, in no uncertain terms, wanted to meet her new grandson. As Johnny started down the stairs, he could see a lady with white hair curled into a bun on top. She was small by no means, and she was smiling from ear to ear as she squeezed Johnny tightly. His mom said something about squeezing the life out of him, but she laughed, and as she did, Johnny could feel what must be love although it did feel a bit like shaking Jello.

His grandmother took his hand and told him she was about to show him around. Johnny was led down the hall to the first-floor kitchen, which was much bigger than the one upstairs. As he looked past the appliances, he could see two windows, and more trees outside! He turned as his grandmother was explaining the dining room. The window there was nearly the size of the front wall and Johnny could see the entire front lawn all the way down to the road. The oak and Maple shaded half of the front property and he couldn't wait to sit beneath the trees, just to daydream.

Johnny turned his attention to a large table which was set for six. He saw plates and glasses, silverware and napkins with napkins rings, cups and saucers. He saw three forks, two knives, and two spoons at each place setting. He had no idea what they were all for, but he did know one thing already. Everything had a place and everything was in its place. As he listened to his grandmother talk about the need for a set table, he could see a China cabinet and a corner cupboard. Both were filled with glasses, cups, and dishes of all colors and sizes. Johnny had never anything like this before. He tried to listen intently even though he would never remember everything that was being said.

As the family walked into the living room, Johnny noticed another giant window. The sun, shining in seemed to lighten up the fireplace, which was on the opposite wall. In front of that was an overstuffed gray chair and an overstuffed sofa. Behind the sofa was a long shelf filled with rocks and shells of all kinds and Johnny knew he would learn about their origins, too. His grandmother began to explain that each rock and shell had come from very special places. They had been collected, over the years, from states both on the east coast and the west coast of the United States. Johnny's mom started laughing and said something about boring Johnny before he even finished the tour of his new home. I guess she had seen Johnny's eyes glass over with all the new information he was receiving.

As Johnny turned to his right, he noticed a bookcase filled with shelf after shelf of books. Next to that was an upright piano and, on the other side of the front door, was a writing desk and chair. None of the furniture really matched, but Johnny could care less. The entire house was the most beautiful thing he had ever seen. All he could do was take in the sight and beam with joy.

After seeing the inside of the house, Johnny asked to go out to the garden to look at the flowers. He went through the side door onto the side porch, passed the rockers, down the four stone steps, and headed to the flowers. When he reached the first flower bed, he stopped in his tracks. There, directly in front of him was a girl picking a rose. She was cute, but that didn't matter to Johnny. Someone was on his new land and she was picking his grandmother's roses. He yelled at her to stop stealing the flowers and told her that she had better leave. After all, this was Johnny's new land and, following all he had learned in the city, he had to protect what was now his.

Upon hearing Johnny shouts and after saying a few choice words, questioning who the heck he thought he was, this strange new girl with blondish hair staired straight through Johnny and pointed a finger at him. She said that she had permission and no boy was going to tell her what to do. She turned and simply ran away. Johnny watched as she left and then went into the house to tell his mother, grandmother, and father what had occurred.

Johnny was taken aback when his mom and dad explained that there had been no need to yell at this girl. They explained to him she was just a neighbor who often came to visit Grandma "T" as she worked in the garden. She was allowed to visit and it was not necessary to chase her off. They assured Johnny that she was used to visiting his grandmother and often helped her dig weeds and, even though he probably didn't feel that way right now, he would end up being friends with her.

Johnny said to himself that there was a fat chance of that. He thought, though, how different country life was going to be. This was going to take some getting used to, for there were no longer alleys and fences and walls separating families like he was accustomed to in the city. Apparently, one was welcomed to walk wherever one wanted and that was the expected way of life here. Sharing, even land, was the thing he was to get used too.

Johnny's mom told him not to worry about what had Happened. She would explain the entire story and what needed to be done later. They would talk about what had just happened to him in a little while, but first it was time to wash up for dinner. Johnny could smell the food as he washed his hands and came to the table. His mom suggested he sit in the chair by the side window. He sat down and his grandmother and mother brought out the food.

He couldn't believe his eyes. There were hot rolls and fried chicken. There was

corn on the cob and green beans. To Johnny, it was a feast fit for a king. Along with the food came lesson number one, though. As he ate, his mother showed him which fork was to be used with which part of the meal. He found out, too, that the spoons were used for different things and there was a butter knife and another knife with which he was to cut his food. He knew it would take so long to memorize what each utensil was for, but he also knew he had all the time he would need to learn it.

After dinner, one of many held in the downstairs dining room and shared by the entire family, came the time for his first lesson. This one was about getting along with neighbors. Johnny's mother and father suggested that the three of them walk to the neighbor's house, introduce their new son, and maybe, Johnny should apologize for yelling and chasing off the girl who lived next door.

He knew he had to say that he was sorry, but when they arrived at the neighbor's front door, he hid a little behind his mom. Johnny listened as he was introduced and shyly said how it was nice to meet them. Under his breath, when he saw the little girl, he kept whispering to himself that it was her alright, it was her. After an apology, Johnny found out that the little girl's name was Judy, He then told her that he was wrong and didn't know better. The most comfortable part of the entire evening situation, for him, was returning home and settling in to his new surroundings.

That night, sleep came easy for Johnny. He was happy and, for the first time in quite a while, he felt safe. He still didn't like the fact that he had to apologize to some girl for what he had done, but that didn't really matter. His new mom sat on the edge of the bed and told him a story. It was a bible story about three men who believed in their God so much, that they refused the wishes of a king. He had demanded they worship his god and reject theirs. They refused and were thrown into a fiery furnace, but were saved by their God. All Johnny could really remember, though, was the strange names of the three characters in the story. He would swear that his mom had given them names to help him sleep with happy thoughts. She had told him they were Shad-rack, Me-Shak, and To-Bed-We-Go. He giggled every time she said their names as quietness took over, and before he knew it, he had fallen to sleep.

It was the smell of frying bacon filled Johnny's room and awakened him early the next morning. His first day in the country had been pretty good, and this new morning was also beginning, for him, to be filled with a great unbelievable joy. Johnny was happy, really happy, for the first time in his entire life. Breakfast was shared by Johnny's mom, Johnny, and his new Grandma T. That is what she preferred to be called and she made sure Johnny knew it. His dad had gone to work, but his mom had taken off from her job as a school counselor, using vacation days to make sure she could be with her new son.

The day was spent riding around Carroll County so that Johnny could see the entire area where lived. He was driven to a place called Reisterstown and taken over what seemed to him to be every road in the county. He and his mom ended up in the city of Westminster and it was there that he helped pick out some groceries that he too would enjoy.

He was even happier later that day when his dad came home from work. As they all sat at the dinner table, Johnny's was asked if he might want to change his name to Price. It was his father that had suggested he may want to take on his name. His grandfather had been William E. Price Senior. His dad was Junior, and Johnny would become William E. the Third. It felt that not only was he accepted as a new member of a new family, he was now being asked to carry one the family name. Johnny said it in his mind four or five times to see how it sounded. William E. Price III - William E. Price III - Will-I-am- E.-Price the third! He was smiling ear to ear when he answered his family in the affirmative. He was happy and he was feeling wanted, really wanted, for the first time in his life.

A new day, a new home, a new family, and, now, a new name. Johnny had no problem saying yes. He wanted it, at that time, more than he had wanted anything. He didn't have to hear a name that hurt or reminded him of a life that had given so much pain. In just a short while, he would no longer be a Johnny. He would be a William, or Billy, for short. It would take less getting used to than anyone thought because for Johnny, he was ready for a change. He was now and forevermore going to be known as William E. Price III.

Chapter 10

Yes, Billy, There is a Santa

It's sad when it takes eight years for a child to realize there just may be a Santa. Johnny, now being called Billy, had heard of other children opening gifts brought by the jolly elf, himself, but had never remembered the joy of a childhood Christmas. If he had received gifts from others, in the past, they were recognizable as hand-me-down toys or clothes. As a matter of fact, Billy never remembered seeing a beautiful decorated Christmas tree and never felt the happiness of putting lights and colorful balls on an evergreen. He had often thought that holidays, special days, and even birthdays were for kids who belonged to a natural family. Foster children, to him, were a group of outcasts who didn't deserve these things, anyway. Now, however, Billy was a part of a real family and he was about to find out what most kids believe to be true. This new family, this new place, this new home brought out an excitement, for Billy, that he had never been a part of before and many surprises were just around the corner. It all started on the fourth Thursday of November. Before Christmas was Thanksgiving dinner which started the season and this Thanksgiving really overwhelmed Billy with a feeling of joy. It was a feeling of being fulfilled both inside and out. The sight of a set table, filled to capacity, was one he had never experienced. His eyes must have been as big as saucers when he looked at this feast. There was a very large turkey stuffed with some kind of a bread mixture. There was corn, beans, potatoes, and gravy. There was this red jelly-like stuff, called cranberry sauce, both homemade and store bought. There were warm buns and butter and, to his delight, there were pies. Not one, but two pies: one was pumpkin and one was apple. Both were fresh and hot, and made Johnny's mouth water.

MOST IMPORTANT, THOUGH, THERE was family. Billy's dad sat at the head of the table. His mom sat to his father's left and next to Billy. Beside him, Grandma T sat laughing and telling everyone one of her stories about how she had almost gotten a ticket for racing a police officer. She explained how she beat the ticket by telling the cop she thought he was one of those young whippersnappers trying to race her. Apparently, the officer was laughing so hard, that he let her go with a warning.

Sitting next to her were Johnny's new Aunt Ellie and Uncle Dan, accompanied by their two children Steve and Danielle. He didn't know them well, and they were just really good friends of his mom and dad, but Billy didn't care. They had grown to be such close friends, they were considered family, anyway. Everyone at the table suddenly got quiet and before they began to eat, a blessing was said, thanking God for all the things He had provided. This was done at every dinner, but it felt a bit more special on this day.

Billy listened intently to all the conversations going on at once. He seemed to have this special gift. He could hear and comprehend the words of more than one person who was speaking at a time. He understood what was being said even though he didn't know the content of some of the conversations. Billy guessed he had learned to do this because of survival. He had to listen to foster parents while still understanding what some of his foster brothers might be saying, in case he needed a forewarning of something bad they had been planning. He could interpret the words of this gathering of family and friends, most of which seemed to be in the form of questions. He would hear his grandmother ask how his Uncle Doc was doing and, at the same time, understand uncle Dan ask What Billy's dad's plans were for the Holidays. His mom was asking if anyone had heard what the town was planning. This was followed by, a statement from his dad telling, Billy, to hold his food over his plate, because Billy was spilling his corn down the front of his shirt. Billy also heard his father tell every one of his plan to get the family tree on Saturday next. He asked Billy if he wanted to go along because he would need help choosing the right tree for them. Of course Billy was all for this. He wanted to be a part of everything.

To him, Christmas became no more than a continuation of Thanksgiving. It was all celebration! When he went with his parents on the first Saturday of December to the town of Westminster, he could see all the stores that had been decorated for the season. The city itself, seemed to take on a beautiful and unbelievable change in the attitude of the people and the joy of a season that was to be shared by all.

Just days before Thanksgiving the town was barren of decorations and on the day after Thanksgiving every street twinkled and shown with lighted trees, bows, and gifts boxes, all in anticipation of the most wonderful season of the year. As Billy's dad drove down Main street, on his way to the buy a tree, Billy could see the streetlights; each was decorated with a wreath that seemed to give the very meaning to the word festive.

From the beginning of Main Street, Billy could the houses and small businesses readying for the celebration. The Westminster Trust Co. simply had a Christmas bow. In front of the Davis Library, Billy swore he saw a jolly man with a long white beard dressed in a red suit. He wondered if maybe this Santa thing was true, all along. Before his dad drove over the railroad tracks, in the middle of the town, he could see the window of Mather's decorated with all kinds of gift ideas. Billy's dad continued to Pennsylvania Avenue where he pulled in front of Dutterer's florist. His dad stopped and went in to by some flowers for Billy's mom.

When they came out Billy's dad asked if he wanted to go look at toys and get ideas for gifts that Santa could bring. Billy nodded his head, even though he wasn't sure this Santa was a real person or not. He wasn't about to ask, though. He didn't want to spoil anything. His dad drove them to the Westminster Shopping Center where Billy saw a store window crammed with toys and electronics.

The store, Joe the Motorists Friend, had a large selection of TV's and tape recorders along with cowboy holster sets for the boys. He, too, looked at the bikes for both boys and girls. Billy was excited, however, to see the trains. His couldn't take his eye off of the sets of Lionel trains. There were freight trains and steamers with smoke, whistles, and real working headlights. He also saw accessories like tracks and tunnels, along with buildings and crossing lights.

Billy didn't want to leave and told his dad that he wanted Santa to bring him a train. His dad told him he was going to be happy, but he might have to choose something else, because they already had two train sets. Billy could hardly wait. He looked around the store and got dozens of ideas of toys he would just love. He had never been involved in such happiness and he felt he was going to burst with joy. He now had ideas for a list he could write to Santa, so then he and his dad decided to go and get the tree.

Billy's dad drove to the spot were Boy Scout Troop 393 was selling Christmas trees. They pulled into the parking lot of the Grace Lutheran Church and began a search. His father had said he always got a real tree, because anything else wouldn't look and smell like Christmas. After they picked out a most beautiful tree and tied it to the roof of the family car, The Price boys went home to transform their house just as the town of Westminster had transformed the streets and businesses.

Billy watched as his dad trimmed the base of the tree so that it would fit just right in their living room. Then came the boxes of Christmas decorations. Billy had never seen so many. There were lights, decorative balls, ornaments, and garland for the inside tree and lights for the outside evergreen and there was even a set for the house itself. Billy had never been a part of such a wonderful time placing lights and colorful balls, garland and even one special ornament, which looked just like Santa, on the tree.

After the tree was decorated, Billy saw another box. This was a specially marked box containing a nativity scene. Inside was a Manger, a Mary and Joseph, shepherds with sheep and a cow, and three Kings complete with camels and three gifts for the Christ child. At the bottom of the box, was the baby Jesus. It almost smiled and, with outstretched arms, centered the entire scene as it was placed on the fireplace mantel.

As if this wasn't enough, Billy's father brought out two large boxes and laid them on the floor, and Billy could see, with mouth opened, the two train sets his dad had told him about. As his father set the controller to the track. He carefully placed the engine on the track, while he made sure to explain why it was called a 2–6-2. Billy listened intently, not wanting to miss a single word. After the engine, Billy's dad placed a coal car, a box car, a log carrier, and a little red caboose.

The second train was placed around the first. It was a bit newer and shined of red and silver. As Billy's dad put together this set, he told Billy that this model was a copy of one on which he had actually traveled. It was called the Santa Fe Super Chief, and it was his favorite. When the building was complete, Billy and his dad laid on the floor, side by side, and watched as both trains traveled the track under the tree. Finally, he realized that this was what Christmas was all about. It was love and hope and joy and true happiness.

Christmas was getting closer and Billy was remembering a little bit of his past. He went to his mother with the question of all questions. He looked down at the floor, expecting a sad answer, when he asked if there really was a Santa Claus. Without missing a beat, Billy's mom got out scrapbookswhich contained newspaper clippings. She opened one and began reading about a little girl named Virginia, who had asked the same question. The story explained how Santa existed. After she finished reading, Billy asked if he had been good enough for Santa to visit him. His mother lifted his chin, looked into his eyes, and told him it was more about love than doing good works, but she was sure that Santa would not skip Billy this year.

As the day came closer and closer, Billy got less and less sleep. Waiting was the hardest thing for a kid who had lived a life of disappointment. The night before the big day, Billy could hardly control himself. He was filled with anticipation and excitement from the beginning of Christmas Eve until his mother tucked him into bed. Somewhere between "there arose such a clatter . . ." and ". . . to all a good night" Billy drifted off to sleep.

On Christmas morning, the only thing up before the sun were the children waiting to see what they had received for Christmas. This year was no different for Billy. When he awoke, he rushed to his mother's and father's room shouting with joy. The sleepy parents followed their son to the living room to see what every parent wanted to see.

This year was not a disappointment to either child or parent. Billy dropped to his knees when he saw more gifts than he had ever seen before anywhere. Some belonged to his mom, some belonged to his dad, some were even marked Grandma T, but there were many with his name written in some unknown and fancy handwriting.

As Billy opened his presents; he thought back to the newspaper article his mother had read to him. He could only think about how this Virginia, whoever she was, was a pretty smart kid, for she had found an answer to a question Billy hadn't even known to ask.

Chapter 11

Change Brings About Change

CHRISTMAS FOLLOWED CHRISTMAS AS Billy grew up and became a young teen in Middle school. All of his past had been forgotten, or purposely hidden in the depths of memory. Sadness, though, as he knew all too well, surrounded him from time to time. His two Grandmothers had passed away and he would remember them as he sat quietly staring off at nothing. He knew people didn't live forever, but no one he had really known had ever died before.

Since his one grandmother had lived in Baltimore, and he hadn't seen her as much, it never affected him as it did when his Grandma T died in a car accident in the late 60's. She had been the grandmother of all grandmothers. She was always helping others and, whenever Billy's mother said no to something he wanted, she would make sure he got it. When Billy's mother would give Grandma T the "evil eye," and scold her a bit saying something about spoiling the boy, Grandma T would giggle and say how she didn't know anything about it. After all, it was the job of every grandmother to spoil her grandchildren. Billy never knew how much he would miss his grandmother! He, staring at nothingness, would feel the sadness of loss, but he also had all the good memories that could bring a smile to his face and she would always live in his heart.

Billy learned about the sadness of death, but he also had learned that it was love that made a family just as much as blood does. His mother had often read him a poem that said he was not necessarily "flesh of her flesh nor bone of her bone," but he was still ". . . miraculously" her own son. He could never remember the author, but that didn't matter. His mom and dad had made Johnny a part of their family, just as if he had been born into it. She had always told him that she was proud he was her real son and that he should never forget that.

His father had always been proud of him, too, even though there were many times that Billy would do things to try his father's patients. He wasn't always good and he often didn't listen, but he always knew forgiveness. Time after time, when Billy had done something wrong and had suffered the consequences, his father would explain why he had done what he had to. He often told Billy that even if he was mad and yelled or had to punish him, that it didn't mean he didn't care. The one thing that really stuck with Billy was that his father only put his hands on him to hug him, or pat him on the head, and never used them to hit him. Billy knew that his dad loved him, even if he didn't always take the time to tell him so.

Billy's dad worked hard to help provide for the family. He worked for years in Baltimore City, at the Fidelity & Guaranty Life Insurance Company or, as he always called it, the Fiddle-Dee-Dee company. He was hardly home, especially during the summer because he would leave early in the morning and get home late at night because it took a much longer time to make it to Baltimore in the 1960's. There were no super highways or four-lane beltways back then connecting the Westminster area to the city of Baltimore. After a hard work week, weekends were saved for cutting grass, resting, and going on visits with family and friends. Sundays always meant church and family dinner. Even though Billy understood why his dad wasn't always around, he wished they had more time together.

Billy's mom worked, too. She was an educator, teaching year after year and eventually becoming one of the counselors at the local high school in Westminster. Even though she worked during the summer vacation for a few weeks, because of her position, she was able to be home basically with the same schedule as Billy, and he loved being with his mom, but he missed his dad. It was only natural, because of this situation, that Billy felt his dad just didn't have much time for him.

When Billy had turned fourteen, his father explained how some things were about to change. The company he worked for was moving to another state and the position he held would no longer be available in Maryland. Billy's dad was choosing not to go with them. Billy was excited, thinking he would now have more time to spend with his father. This, however, was not going to be the case.

Billy's mother continued counseling, but had started a guidance program at the elementary school level, while his dad went back to school. He learned a trade he had always wished for, and when he graduated he started his own business. He opened up a transmission shop and worked long hours as his clientele increased. The more work that came in, the less time Billy's dad had to share with him.

Holidays were still wonderful, dinners were still a shared time together, and Sundays were the only day that work ceased and the family went to church. Somehow, however, Billy and his dad seemed to grow a little bit apart. When Billy was doing his chores or completing his homework, or practicing his cornet, he would receive the approving pat on the head or the usual "good job, boy,"

Billy loved his dad and he knew his dad loved him, but there was less communication as he grew older. Now, being in High school meant sharing time with friends, after-school parties, dances, and games of football with the neighborhood kids. That took the place of family time, and Billy and his dad grew even further apart and had less in common. Sometimes, Billy thought that his dad loved his shop more than he loved him.

Deep inside he knew his dad loved and cared for him, but a kid is not inclined to think that deeply. Thoughts, at this age, are actually pretty selfish for any boy and many times "I" becomes more important than "we". Time, though, has a way of showing the importance of life that is to be shared and not taken for granted, and time was about to teach Billy a lesson.

Chapter 12

A Christmas to Remember

FIFTEEN IS AN AWKWARD age for any boy. There are so many changes going on at once. Billy was no different than other boys his age. Pressures at school, hormones pushing and pulling in every direction, meeting new friends and losing others, all combining to make for a life full of confusions. One minute there was nothing but happiness and success and the next there were miseries and failures, each causing different emotions. At times, this would made Billy think that the world was crashing down around him. He was having some problems with school work, but with a little more study and some after school help from his teachers, Billy got by. He wasn't a horrible student, but he wasn't at the top of his class either.

Each troubling situation affected Billy and sometimes he thought he would just not survive them. His mom used to call these predicaments "Hemlock Mountains", which was probably another allusion to some line in some book she had read to him in the past. If a problem arose and it solved itself or it was solved because of intervention, Billy's mother would always tell him that they made it over another Hemlock Mountain. Some successes were pretty easy, while others were painfully hard, but none were impossible until that Christmas just before Billy turned sixteen.

The entire year before that Christmas, Billy and his dad barely communicated. Sometimes there were days where they didn't even see much of each other, even though they were only a few hundred yards apart at any given time.

This had made Billy think that maybe his father didn't care for much of anything other than the success of his own business. His mother often told him that the family was the reason that his dad worked so hard, but boys don't always look at life through logical glasses. No connection meant no communication and no communication meant no caring.

At the time, Billy didn't know how wrong he was going to be. It had been said many times in his life that one never misses the water until the well runs dry, but Billy never realized the importance of this proverb, and he had no reason to until this particular holiday. Thanksgiving had been, once again, a great time with family and friends. There was good food, Aunts and Uncles, and many things for which Billy should be grateful. . . and for the most part, he was. Christmas vacation began with excitement and anticipation. That year the crisp cold air and the early wintry weather created a need for time spent inside more than out. Billy got off the school bus on the last day before his vacation and went directly into the house, placing his book-bag on the couch and sat down looking at the Christmas tree. His mother was not yet home, so he walked outside to his dad's garage to see what work was going on there. He stood at the door of the shop and the distinct smell of transmission fluid filling the air. He said hi to his dad and started to walk toward a car, high on the lift. He noticed the transmission on the side and parts boxes on the floor.

His father greeted him with what seemed like a grunt, and ask Billy to watch out for the mess on the floor, explaining how he didn't want him tracking it around on his shoes. He followed up by saying something about just not having the time to get up the mess. The words jumbled together, for Billy, as he watched his father putting new pieces back into the transmission. Billy observed the scene for a few more minutes, until he heard his mother come into the driveway. He turned to walk out, half listening to his dad say something about how he should go and help his mom.

As Billy walked to the car, he could see his mom taking packages out of the trunk. He couldn't see what was in the bags, but not for the trying. Billy's mom gave him the usual talk about not being so nosy during the holiday season. Handing him a bag of groceries, she told him he should go inside and put them away for her, smiling as she did so. Billy walked into the house, heading toward the kitchen and began putting away the contents of the bag.

After his mom entered, he expressed to her how he didn't understand why his dad didn't have time for him. He told her about the times he went into the garage and the many times he was chased out. He listened to her, as she tried to explain how hard his dad worked and that, if Billy thought his father didn't care, he was wrong. It had nothing to do with him and one day he would understand.

The entire week before Christmas went about the same as that day when Billy had gotten off the bus. His dad went out early to work in the shop and his mom spent her time making cookies and pies, as well playing secret Santa in her bedroom. Billy tried to peek, but never got away with it. She was way too aware of his antics and she was way too good at hiding presents. She constantly told Billy he had to learn patience and often said it in the form of a poem, so Billy would never forget. "Patience is a virtue. Possess it if you can. Seldom found in women and never found in men." Then she would laugh and give him a hug. It was yet another quote that Billy had no idea who had authored it or where it originated, but it didn't matter to him. His mom always had a way of teaching him with a smile and, given the way he felt about his father having no time for him, he appreciated that. Christmas morning was like every Christmas morning in Billy's household. He was always the first to awaken. It didn't matter that he was a teenager, Christmas was Christmas, and as far as he was concerned, everyone, no matter how old, was a child on Christmas day. Billy almost ran to his mom's and dad's bedroom to announce that Christmas had finally arrived. He roused his parents and they followed him to the living room.

There, under the tree, was gift upon gift. For the first time there were even two presents from Billy to his mom and dad. Because he had worked for the past year, delivering the Grit newspaper, Billy had saved enough to buy his parents a little gift and he was proud of that. After all, he had been taught that this season was the season of giving. And it felt good, too. Christmas was indeed a miracle that happened every 25th of December, and everyone, even for just a day, became a little nicer, a little kinder, a little more childlike. Billy went for his stocking, as he always had, and carried that to the dining room table. It was a yearly tradition and it wasn't about to change. Every year, he would take his stocking and view its contents as his mother made cinnamon buns. His dad would sit with him at the table and watch. No unwrapping of gifts would ever be done before the cinnamon buns, milk, and coffee.

When the family finished the traditional Christmas morning breakfast, Billy raced to the living room to see his presents. This year, he opened the usual socks and clothes gifts first. Then, each one of the three took turns opening the remaining gifts, oohing and awing and thanking the giver. Billy enjoyed the gifts and was always thankful, but this year the pile seemed a little smaller than the past. He knew there had to be something else because his dad was smiling from ear to ear, and this hardly ever happened. He couldn't imagine why his father took him by the hand and led him to the basement door telling him he had one more surprise.

Billy was carefully led down into the basement and stood on the bottom step. His jaw must have dropped to the floor as he remained there unable to move. He just kept staring in disbelief at this Christmas gift that outdid any other gift he had ever received. His father asked him if he like it and Billy shouted something that sort of sounded somewhat like, "Like it, I love it." Wow followed wow as he looked at the beautiful pool table sitting in front of him. He saw the rack and the balls and the sticks and he walked over to the table placing his hands on the green felt top.

His dad told him that he was about to teach him a lesson in humility, but Billy could care less about winning or losing, He was so happy that he and his father were playing together and that this one Christmas gift was the one that would eliminate his feeling of division. He and his father played game after game, laughing and making jokes, and stopping only to eat lunch and dinner. What a Christmas this had been! This one was the one that meant more than any other to Billy.

That night, as he drifted off to sleep, he knew he would dream of the many games he and his father would share in the future. This one gift, this pool table, was much more than a present. It was a connection between father and son that could not be broken. It wasn't about the expense, and Billy knew it had to have cost quite a bit. It was simply that he had a glimpse of that which he had been so wrong about. His mom had tried to explain and until this moment, Billy had not understood. His dad was a man that cared. He didn't always know how to show it . . . but, without a doubt, he cared.

Chapter Final

The Day That Changed his World

BILLY WOKE UP IN the morning after Christmas wanting to ask his father when they could play another game of pool. After he got dressed, he looked in his parent's room, but it was empty. He went to the dining room and then to the kitchen. Both were almost too quiet. He next stopped in the basement, taking a little time to touch the felt on the pool table top and to roll a ball into the corner pocket. He thought back to the fantastic present and all that it meant to him. It was indeed the gift that had brought him together with his father. But, the basement, too, was an empty place. Billy walked up the stairs and to the front door. He opened it looking to see if anyone was in the garage, but it was locked. He looked for his mother's and father's car, but noticed that both cars were gone.

Billy had figured that his parents had gone out for a cup of coffee. His dad, especially, would leave, sometimes, early in the morning, to have coffee at the local Finksburg pharmacy with the "boys" as he called them. He shared his free time with another mechanics and the pharmacist at the lunch counter even though the counter, itself, never saw a lunch customer until ten or eleven.

Billy never went, but he knew his dad's friends. There was "Spence", who owned his own engine shop, near Westminster, and shared some business with Billy's dad. There was also "Skip", the pharmacist who told more jokes than anyone Billy knew. Usually, his mother would not tag along with his dad, saying it was a guy thing, but Billy figured the house was empty today because it was the Christmas Holiday. He just had a feeling that the two of them would be home at any second. Billy walked to the television and decided to watch a few cartoons until his parents returned.

As Bugs Bunny cartoons changed to Road Runner, Billy began to constantly look out the window for the return of his parents. As the minutes passed, Billy began to worry. It wasn't the norm for both of his parents to be gone at the same time, and he began to feel uncomfortable about the situation. Finally, he heard a car coming up the driveway. It had taken more than hour since he had started watching cartoons for the door to open. Billy's mom walked in with his Aunt Ellie and Uncle Dan. He could see that she had been crying and, as she sat down on the couch, she began to shake. Billy rushed to her and asked what was wrong. She grabbed him and held him tighter than he could ever remember her doing before.

Through tears, she kept saying, over and over again that he was gone. A message about a death takes little time to sink in. Emotion seems to develop directly from the brain, affecting the stomach, knotting it up, and almost immediately turning the eyes to tears. Billy began to cry as he asked his uncle what was going on. Billy's Uncle Dan knelt down and softly told Billy that his father had suffered a massive heart attack and had passed away. He was gone. Billy would not - could not, believe what he was being told. There was no way. His father, just a few weeks ago, had gotten a clean bill of health and there was just no way he could have died. Uncle Dan tried to comfort Billy by explaining that his dad felt nothing as he fell onto the Pharmacy floor. It had all happened so quickly.

The first question on Billy's mind was why. His world had come crashing down on him the day after he and his dad had shared something for the very first time. It was supposed to be a different world, where dad and son spent many times playing and sharing and, finally, communicating. This was now impossible and Billy wanted to know why. Why! He ran to his room and fell to his bed crying and shouting at the same time.

He questioned God, himself, and wondered if he had to bear some of the responsibility for this horrible event. The entire day was a blur and nothing made sense. The whole world felt as if it had been turned upside down. Billy remained in his bed until his Aunt called to him and asked him to come out and maybe get a little bite to eat, but Billy said he wasn't hungry. Naturally, he had lost his appetite, and everyone understood, telling him maybe he would want something later. He did come out of his room, though, and sit at the table. In front of him was a sandwich and some chips that Aunt Ellie had fixed for him. He first stared at the food and then he could do nothing but stare out of the dining room window. Finally, Billy's mom took away his full plate, knowing he would eat when he was ready. Tears and thoughts seemed to run together throughout the entire day. At one point, Billy walked to the basement and sat crying in front of the pool table. Every stick he touched and every pool ball he rolled into a pocket reminded him of the happiness he had experienced and, now, had been taken from him. He still wondered if he had been better or kinder somehow to his dad, things would have been different. Billy slowly put away the pool cues and went back upstairs. He spent most of the day in silence, and soon bedtime crept up on him. After he was ready for bed, his mother came, as she had often done, to tuck him in for the night. Billy seemed to be all cried out, but still in shock. He finally told his mom he thought that maybe this was somewhat his fault. Billy was trying to ask his mom all the questions racing through his brain, but nothing else would come out. She held him and assured him that nothing he had done caused this. She explained how everyone was given a certain time to live and, even though we would never really fully understand, we all must go through this pain and learn from it.

Billy didn't fully comprehend, but he seemed a bit calmer as she spoke. She explained, also, how things might have been if Billy and his dad had not had that Christmas together. What depth of sadness would Billy have to endure if there had been no time for him and his father to share, laugh, and play together. The greatest gift Billy ever got was given in that moment between answers and tears. It had nothing to do with him; it was a time to remember the love and not the pain.

Billy's mom left for a moment and came back with a poetry book. She told him she wanted him to listen to a poem that explained what she had believed all her life and hoped that maybe it would help Billy. She began to read and he listened intently to a poem written by poet Alfred Lord Tennyson.

> *Sunset and evening star, And one clear call for me!*
> *And may there be no moaning of the bar, When I put out to sea,*

Billy's mom stopped after the first verse and explained to him how the author was writing about someone was going on a trip and those he was leaving should not cry when he was gone. She then continued.

> *But such a tide as moving seems asleep, Too full for sound and foam,*
> *When that which drew from out the boundless deep, turns again home.*

Billy's mother further explained that the speaker wanted what should be an easy quiet voyage and that the outgoing tide would take him to his new home peacefully. She continued by reading the next verse.

> *Twilight and evening bell, And after that the dark!*
> *And may there be no sadness of farewell, When I embark;*

Billy interrupted and told her he understood. The person in the poem was leaving this world and heading into the darkness of death. Billy added that he didn't want everyone crying for him when he died. His mom smiled as she finished the poem.

For Tho' from out our bourne of Time and Place, The flood may bear me far,
I hope to see my Pilot face to face, When I have crossed the bar.

Billy smiled too, for the first time since hearing the news. He looked at the lady that had helped change his entire life; the one he was blessed enough to call mom. Billy, with eyes half- closed, understood then, that his dad, like the speaker in this poem, was on his way to meet his creator, and this trip would carry him to God. There would still be tears, but every day a bit less pain. Billy drifted off, a bit calmer and a little more secure.

From that night on, Billy was a different person. He not only felt different inside, but he had a different attitude showing on the outside. Billy had gone through a life of incredible pain while being treated as an outcast, beaten, and abused. He learned to live without emotion and almost without a heart, but he had survived. He had become a part of a family who had chosen him, not because of birth, but because of love. No matter what had happened in Billy's life, the answer lay in that one-word Love - a love that God had given for all true families to try and follow. More importantly, though, he had been given the opportunity to see what life could have been without it, and with one Hemlock Mountain after another, he realized the true meaning of family and unconditional love.

Appendix

Crossing the Bar

Sunset and evening star,
And one clear call for me!
And may there be no moaning of the bar,
When I put out to sea,

But such a tide as moving seems asleep,
Too full for sound and foam,
When that which drew from out the boundless deep
Turns again home.

Twilight and evening bell,
And after that the dark!
And may there be no sadness of farewell,
When I embark;

For tho' from out our bourne of Time and Place
The flood may bear me far,
I hope to see my Pilot face to face
When I have cross'd the bar.

Alfred, Lord Tennyson (1889)

An Adoption Poem

Not flesh of my flesh,
nor bone of my bone
but very remarkably,
all my own.
And never forget,
for a single minute,
that you weren't born
under my heart,
but in it.

Attributed to Fleur Conkling Heyliger

About the Author

To the author, *Bill Price*, words tell a story and paint a picture or a movie in the mind of the reader. Many times he would say picture may be worth a thousand words, but it is words that can create a picture. In *The Biography Of Little Johnny L. Mitchell*, the author recounts his memories growing up in the foster care system. He shares what happened to some young children who were forced to be shuffled from home to home in the 1950's and the 1960's.

He explains how the lack of care and how true family love shapes a young life. As seen through the eyes of a child, he explains what happens when that child finds a "real" family and finally defines real love. He learns, from experience to experience, that a family's love is what is important and he finally gets a chance to experience it.

www.ingramcontent.com/pod-product-compliance
Lightning Source LLC
LaVergne TN
LVHW020652100826
845148LV00012B/2442

* 9 7 9 8 3 8 5 2 7 3 0 9 6 *